OBJECTS OF WAR

OBJECTS OF WAR
CURRENCY IN A TIME OF CONFLICT

Kevin Clancy

Foreword by Sir Hew Strachan

Frontispiece: Clay model by sculptor Paul Day for a United Kingdom First World War commemorative coin issued in 2018.

First published in Great Britain in 2018
by the Royal Mint Museum and Spink & Son Ltd

Royal Mint Museum, Llantrisant, Pontyclun CF72 8YT
www.royalmintmuseum.org.uk

Spink & Son Ltd, 67-69 Southampton Row, London WC1B 4ET
www.spink.com

The moral right of Kevin Clancy to be identified as the author of
this work has been asserted by him in accordance with the Copyright,
Designs and Patents Act of 1988

Images copyright as attributed
All other images and text © Crown copyright 2018

All coins are reproduced at actual size unless otherwise stated
Banknotes have not been reproduced at actual size for security reasons

ISBN 978-1-907427-90-9

A CIP catalogue record for this book is available from
the British Library

Designed by Tuch, London
Printed and bound in Wales by Cambrian Printers, Aberystwyth

Foreword

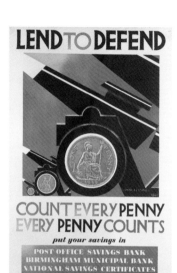

LEND TO DEFEND

COUNT EVERY PENNY EVERY PENNY COUNTS

put your savings in

**POST OFFICE SAVINGS BANK
BIRMINGHAM MUNICIPAL BANK
NATIONAL SAVINGS CERTIFICATES**

Above and right. Posters encouraging members of the public to invest in war loans (above, © IWM) from the Second World War and (right) from the First World War.

Carl von Clausewitz famously defined war as the continuation of policy by other means. In doing so, he seemed to de-emphasise its power to precipitate change. This is misleading: states which start wars frequently do so because they are not happy with the status quo. Moreover, war itself is a powerful and even revolutionary force for innovation. That has been particularly true in relation to war's effects on economics and finance (a topic on which Clausewitz had nothing to say). The establishment in early modern Europe of centralised states which monopolised armed force, and so legitimised themselves by providing domestic security for their peoples and defence against their enemies, depended on money. Standing armed forces had to be paid, as did the contractors who supplied them and the artisans who made their equipment. A well-ordered army, when in the field, bought its supplies rather than plundered them. So war promoted both the use of cash and its circulation. A state's coinage was as representative of its power as were the soldiers and sailors who wore its uniforms. Moreover, the state recouped its disbursements, at least in part, by taxing the money which it distributed for goods and services. Income tax in Britain is in origin a war tax.

Kevin Clancy's *Objects of War* highlights these interlocking relationships. In doing so it serves to remind us that, although war may precipitate change, war's history contains features that are recurrent. Dr Clancy is Director of the Royal Mint Museum, and so, logically enough, coinage is at the centre of his book. His thematic structure brings out, in lively and engaging prose, persistent themes in the role of finance in war: its function in supporting allies, its capacity to create inflation and so erode a belligerent from within, and the preference for specie when confidence in notes is loosened. Dr Clancy reminds us, as we ponder the future of Europe and the euro, how much common currencies with international convertibility are the products of peace, and depend upon it for their survival. War's capacity is to disrupt and divide, frequently forcing belligerent states to develop or adapt their own coinage just as much as to raise their own forces.

However, our understanding of these links has become weaker, particularly since the end of the Cold War and its so-called 'peace dividend'. In 2008 Joseph Stiglitz, winner of a Nobel prize in economics, put the cost to the United States alone of the ongoing war in Iraq at $3 trillion. That same year western economies crashed, in large part because of excessive and unsecured debt. States in the past, which failed to manage the transition from war to peace by addressing the borrowing which war generated, could pay a heavy domestic political price: in 1789 the accumulated costs of war generated revolution in France, and after 1918 hyperinflation eroded the authority of republican Germany. Although neither the United States nor the United Kingdom had introduced special taxes to pay for the wars in Iraq and Afghanistan, nobody attributed the 2008 economic crash to the unsecured costs of the fighting. This was an extraordinary, if largely unnoticed, break with the past. It meant that the west's sense of its own security, and its expectation of persistent economic well-being, were not eroded by its wars of intervention or its fear of terrorism. Neither George W. Bush nor Barack Obama saw political value in highlighting the real economic costs of America's wars. As a result the peoples of the 'west' have neglected the links between war and finance. Past generations, especially in Britain, were wont to speak of the power of silver bullets, of finance as a weapon of war in its own right. Today the public tends to see the cost of war almost exclusively in terms of blood, rather than of treasure. Here, as elsewhere, Donald Trump has broken the mould, consistently stressing the economic burden shouldered by the United States through its contribution to NATO and the accumulated costs of its war in Afghanistan. Will his reminder of war's costs, however selectively interpreted, prove to be an isolated phenomenon or has he the capacity to re-open a neglected debate?

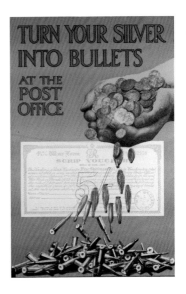

Sir Hew Strachan

Introduction

During the war in the Balkans in the 1990s a journalist covering the conflict relayed the story of locals going out for a drink and always buying two bottles of beer instead of one because by the time they had drunk the first the second would have gone up in price. It may have been somewhat embellished in the re-telling but the reality of war causing rapid increases in prices and a related fall in the value of a currency is far from unusual. War has shaped currencies by creating, abolishing and re-moulding them. It is a relationship as old as money itself and, while conflict and currencies exist in their own spheres and are driven by forces peculiar to themselves, they have nevertheless walked the same paths on many occasions.

Right. Print by artist Justine Smith titled *Collateral Damage*, 2007. (Courtesy of Justine Smith.)

Successful currencies thrive on stability, whereas war is born of disagreement and disruption to the normal patterns of life. It is, perhaps, the sense in which coins and banknotes bind communities and have created links between cultures that makes them such a poignant casualty of war. A military commander requires currency to mobilise his troops and yet the very thing he needs can on occasion buckle under the strain of the war he is fighting. Beyond such tensions there are deep-seated human instincts involved. When lives are threatened by advancing troops an insurance policy has often been taken out in the form of a spade with which to dig a hole to hide what is precious and quite often what is precious turns out to have been gold and silver coins. Some time later, when the soldiers have packed up and gone home, the hope was to recover the buried treasure. Many did. Some did not and we have in the eventual retrieval of such hoards the physical evidence of the panic war induces.

From the perspective of the advancing generals a currency can become a means to reinforce victory. In the second half of the twentieth century reports of revolutionaries taking control of a country would often include details of how they headed straight for the television or radio station to broadcast news of their success. Regime change can also be declared through a re-design of coins and notes. A little more time elapses but the intention is the same.

As well as being hidden in the ground or placed in the vanguard of a new leader's identity, currencies have been debased or withdrawn entirely; access to bullion to make coins has been restricted or there have been unexpected windfalls in supply; those actually making currencies have had to increase output to meet demand and the amount of paper money issued has sometimes spiralled out of control; behavioural shifts, too, are part of the story, with coins taking on the role of life-saving shields or being transformed into precious tokens of family and home. Whether in the ranks of the mercenary armies of the Thirty Years War or the battles of the American War of Independence, in the civil unrest of revolutionary

France or in the trenches of the First World War, there is evidence
of how currencies have been either the victims of conflict or its
redoubtable ally, colouring narratives and at times adding tension
to an already chaotic situation. How it looks, how it is made, how
much is needed and who uses it - these staples of stable money
open themselves up for challenge and debate.

By providing the means through which wars have been fought,
coins and banknotes have been indispensable weapons,
occasionally even literally, but how money is raised, how a war
is financed and paid for over time, are closely related matters.
The financial support an army needs to mobilise has shifted from
precious metal coins to sophisticated financial instruments and
as a result the way in which war is paid for has needed to realign.
Although the intention here will be to look at the actual currencies,
the physical form of money and how it has interacted with conflict,
the interwoven narratives of finance and cash will not be neglected.

Tempting as it might be to embark upon a history of war and
currency in its entirety, this volume has no such ambitions. While
stories and evidence from other countries will intrude from time
to time, the limit of this current narrative will largely focus on the
experience of Britain and be confined mostly to the last 500 years.
The approach taken has been thematic in order to draw attention
to patterns that seem to emerge from the subject matter and a
certain amount of cross-referencing has, therefore, necessarily
been employed.

As documents of history currencies have provided many objects
of war and although the historical record has been abundantly
supplemented in recent centuries, money in its broadest sense
can be instructive still in understanding war. The purpose here
is to unlock some of the stories these objects have to tell us and
to inhabit for a moment or two the lives of the people who
made and used them.

THE FIRST WORLD WAR 1914-1918

"YOUR COUNTRY NEEDS.."
YOU

2014

1 Action this day

*He who wishes to fight
must first count the cost.*

Sun Tzu

Right. Photograph of Lloyd George in 1913, Chancellor of the Exchequer at the beginning of the First World War. (© National Portrait Gallery, London.)

One of Winston Churchill's touch-stone phrases during the Second World War was 'Action this Day'. It was, self-evidently, his way of stimulating the need for decisions to be implemented swiftly and he used it so regularly that red labels bearing the words were printed for him to attach to documents. Matters relating to the management of coins and notes in circulation cannot have risen all that high in his priorities when set against strategic concerns but, all the same, they could not be ignored. Instilling a belief amongst the population that there would be sufficient quantities of currency during war was important and in times of peace it is no less a responsibility of government to ensure access to cash. Churchill's urgency to act resonates strongly with what actually happened twenty-five years earlier at the start of the First World War in relation to Britain's currency, contrasting sharply with the leisurely progress of currency reform more usually encountered in peacetime.

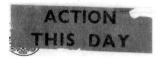

The immediate crisis

It was the summer of 1914 and the need for 'Action this Day' was in the hands of the Chancellor of the Exchequer, Lloyd George. In the weeks following the assassination of Archduke Franz Ferdinand on 28th June tensions between European powers had been growing and as an instinctive defence mechanism banks sought to keep hold of their gold reserves by paying out five-pound notes rather than gold sovereigns. Rumours started to circulate that cast doubt on the solvency of the banking system and on 30th July queues of agitated customers formed outside the Bank of England seeking payment for their notes in gold. From dawn till dusk the Bank's bullion yard was thronged with crowds corralled by harassed warding staff. The same was experienced in Germany, with banks wanting their customers to accept notes rather than gold and account holders demanding exactly the opposite. To avert a serious run on the Bank of England's gold reserves the government had to act and, by extending the early August bank holiday by three days, as well as holding meetings at the Treasury lasting long into the night, enough time was found to agree measures designed to shore up confidence in

Above. Action this Day tag signifying an urgent issue identified by Winston Churchill. (Crown copyright.)

Right. Proof one pound note prepared as an emergency issue by the Bank of England in advance of the First World War but never released. (© Governor and Company of the Bank of England.)

the system. Policies that in times of peace would have taken months if not years to debate and decide were now being approved and set in place with exceptional haste. Amongst a number of connected expedients, it was agreed low denomination notes should be issued immediately and the people of Britain were strongly urged to stop using gold coins for everyday transactions. Britain declared war on Germany on 4th August and when the banks reopened three days later, to the relief of government, the expected demand for cash in gold did not materialise.

The pace of change was breathtaking but in the atmosphere of strained international relations during the weeks and months leading up to the crisis of that summer bank holiday, the Bank was prudent enough to start making preparations by designing a one pound note as an emergency issue. In the event, the paper currency solution materialised as ten shilling and one pound notes, equivalents for the half-sovereign and sovereign, issued in the name of the Treasury not the Bank to promote their circulation in Scotland and Ireland. The pound note was first released on Friday 7th August, with the

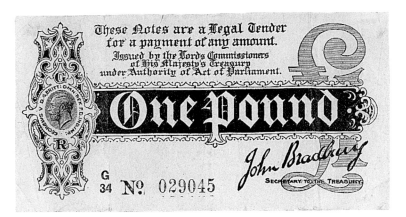

Left. The first issue of Treasury one pound notes, popularly known as Bradburys.
(© Governor and Company of the Bank of England.)

Above. Newspapers gave prominent notice in late July 1914 of the Stock Exchange's closure on account of the growing international tension. (© Hulton Archive/Getty Images.)

Right. Pre-First World War gold sovereigns, enlarged.

ten-shilling note appearing a week later. They came to be nicknamed 'Bradburys' after the Chief Secretary to the Treasury, John Bradbury, whose signature appeared prominently on them as a mark of authority and reassurance to the public. Printed on flimsy paper normally reserved for postage stamps and hurriedly designed by Sir Frederick Atterbury, Controller of the Stationery Office, in his drawing room over the bank holiday weekend, users could have been forgiven for being less than impressed. Nevertheless, the notes were accepted from the outset. Paper currency of a similar nature, although designed to a much higher standard, was issued in Germany and, in being positioned as an equivalent or replacement for gold, fulfilled a comparable function. Taking prompt action was evident in Austria-Hungary, too, as shown in an order being placed on 23rd July to strike 400 million crowns to meet the army's immediate cash needs.

As far as the coinage was concerned, Lloyd George's patriotic plea for people to stop using gold sovereigns found a receptive audience and from that point on the many centuries of familiarity with the everyday use of gold in the markets and high-streets of Britain started to come to an end.

The measures meant, in effect, the suspension of the Bank Charter Act of 1844 which fixed the ratio between gold and the Bank of England's note issues. It had operated successfully as a mechanism for shoring up the gold reserves of the Bank but the advent of war challenged that equilibrium. From a low point in the summer of 1914 of £10 million, the reserves had recovered quickly as a result of the action taken and by December of that year were back up to £51.8 million. The release of Treasury notes was directed at creating liquidity in the system and addressing internal demand for gold but the economist John Maynard Keynes argued at the time that Britain should continue to meet its international trade obligations in gold to reinforce its credit status with other countries. Maintaining convertibility internationally was, to him, essential and Lloyd George eventually came to accept the position which resulted

in a gold exchange standard operating between, for example, Britain, the United States and France. The outbreak of war was a disaster for the intricate network of mutually supportive banking and trading relationships linking countries together but, despite all the pressures war brought, none of the great financial institutions collapsed. In large part this was because of decisiveness in the face of a crisis, but the impact *was* felt on individual currencies (Chapter 7, pp. 119-21).

A new and better quality version of the Bradbury one pound note was released in the autumn of 1914, presaging an extended conflict, and the closure of the London Stock Exchange throughout the remainder of the year, not re-opening until 4th January 1915, was a further indication of continuing anxiety in financial markets. The way in which the onset of war impacted on matters relating to the currency shifted in time and was felt no less severely right across Europe but what is distinctive about the days leading up to the start of hostilities was the political instinct to preserve stability, or some vestige of it, because without this the financial means required to conduct the war would have been undermined. New currency arrangements were introduced under the shadow of a grave threat and even the abandonment of the gold standard itself, at least from a domestic point of view, was judged a price worth paying. What is also noteworthy about this episode is the similarity it bears to a military crisis against a different European power Britain confronted 117 years earlier.

The setting was Fishguard in west Wales. Revolutionary France had declared war on Britain in 1793 and, following threats of a French invasion, in February 1797 a group of 1,400 French troops landed with the objective of converting what they thought would be sympathetic Welsh locals to the revolutionary cause. The hapless band, it transpired, were less than enthusiastic about their mission and they were soon rounded up. In other circumstances that might have been the end of the matter. News of the military pantomime,

however, travelled quickly and morphed into talk of a full-scale invasion, the resulting unease sending large numbers to banks to secure the release of their gold. That the threat was unfounded was not the point. Hysteria, once whipped up, generated its own momentum and began to risk eroding the Bank of England's ability to give gold in exchange for its notes. Government had to act and, as in August 1914, policy was agreed and implemented on the spot.

The preamble to this moment of monetary high drama was characterised by decades of prevarication over how or even whether to reform the silver coinage and what to do about the large issues of unofficial copper tokens and counterfeits widely circulating in most parts of the country. It is said that the Prime Minister, William Pitt, passed a whole night pacing up and down his drawing room reflecting on what to do. The result of Pitt's late-night deliberations, and other discussions with colleagues, was to authorise an emergency issue of Spanish silver coins, counter-stamped with a small bust of George III, place a long-awaited contract for the production of official copper coins with Matthew Boulton's mint in Birmingham, relieve the Bank of England of its obligation to redeem its notes in gold

Above. Cartwheel penny of 1797 made at Matthew Boulton's mint at Soho, Birmingham.

Right. Bank of England one pound note, dated 1798, issued under the emergency authority arising from the financial crisis of 1797. (© Governor and Company of the Bank of England.)

and permit the circulation of lower denomination banknotes of two pounds and one pound.

From 1797 the war with France lasted a further eighteen years and over that time the elements of Pitt's monetary policy met with varying degrees of success. Allowing the Bank to suspend payment of its notes in cash was extended periodically, justified on the grounds of the circumstances the country confronted, and actually remained in place until 1821, well beyond the end of hostilities. A greater role for banknotes often meant paper currency was being handled for the first time which gave counterfeiters an opportunity to circulate forged notes, undermining confidence in this type of money. Guineas fell out of active circulation, a reality captured by a satirical cartoonist who depicted a banker startled when a guinea was passed across his counter, so rare a sight in circulation had they become. Boulton's copper proved to be extremely popular, with worn specimens turning up many decades later pointing to a coinage actively used. As for the circulation of countermarked Spanish dollars, when their face value was pitched at an appropriate level they were a useful addition to the silver coinage. Evidence of such a tolerance extending towards an overseas currency in times of war was nothing new. Charles I (1625-49), some 150 years earlier during his struggle against Parliament, proclaimed several foreign coins to be legal tender, including the ducatoon and the crosse dollar, large silver coins brought over from the Spanish Netherlands, quite possibly under instruction from Charles' wife, Queen Henrietta Maria.

What was decided over the course of a few days at the end of February and the beginning of March 1797 defined Britain's monetary policy for a generation, and the measures were sustained on the grounds of living through a long and arduous conflict. When England had found itself at war with France 100 years earlier, at the end of the seventeenth century, the

Above. Marble bust of William Pitt by Joseph Nollekens, 1806. William Pitt was Prime Minister of Britain during the crisis of 1797. (© Governor and Company of the Bank of England.)

circumstances of reform were attended with slightly less drama than in the situations just mentioned but the reality of conflict driving the agenda was no less evident.

Reform during war

The war had started in 1688 and had progressively taken its toll on the English economy. Prices had risen and as the rates at which silver and gold changed hands on the bullion market ratcheted up so the currency came under increasing pressure. Older coins, made using the traditional hand-struck method, were clipped savagely, causing a critical loss of confidence in sterling. For William III (1689-1702) the need to initiate a recoinage to restore the value and reputation of England's currency was directly linked to his war against Louis XIV (1643-1715). Legislation was, accordingly, introduced in 1696 and a costly reform embarked upon at a moment when the country could ill afford it. The timing of the recoinage, dictated by the military situation rather than the preparedness of the Mint, created a short-term liquidity crisis but once this had been worked through the decision to recoin could be judged a wise one in light of the international position. In the longer term, however, the consequences of the Great Recoinage were much less favourable for the reputation of sterling, resulting ultimately in too little silver being produced throughout the greater part of the eighteenth century. Taking a firm position on re-establishing the existing standard of silver was partly driven by the memory of the coinage being debased under Henry VIII (1509-47), and partly by John Locke's theories on money and property, but it is not entirely fanciful to think of this policy in terms of England wanting to project itself as strong and defiant at a time of war.

In these three instances, stretching across some 200 years, action was being taken to restore stability or to pre-empt circumstances thought highly likely to create uncertainty or even panic. They are each defining moments in the history of Britain's currency, forming part of the long narrative of the adoption and operation of the gold

Above. Coins produced during the Great Recoinage, including a shilling struck at the temporary mint in Norwich marked with an N below the effigy of William III.

Left. Painting of William III by Sir Godfrey Kneller. (© Governor and Company of the Bank of England.)

standard and, at key moments, they also reveal the power of the military imperative. That these reforms happened when they did stemmed from the conflict at hand and the details of the changes introduced were heavily coloured by the drama of the time.

There have, however, been plenty of other conflicts in which Britain was engaged during this period that did not have, as a by-product, changes to the currency. Then there are instances of currency reform blissfully unencumbered by the sound of guns, whether influenced by the periodic discovery of substantial quantities of bullion or the vicissitudes of economic life. The major recoinage in England in 1279 orchestrated by Edward I (1272-1307), for example, was directed at renewing the coinage rather than being stimulated by any kind of military necessity, while it was the unearthing of gold and silver by the Portuguese and Spanish from the fifteenth century in the new world, rather than any particular battle or war, that was, arguably, the single most important force of the age in transforming the coinages of western Europe. Between the beginning of the sixteenth century and the 1970s there have, by one estimation, been 119 wars involving one or other of the major world powers, which equates to a war every five years or so. Looked at another way, no period of twenty-five years over these 500 years has been entirely without war. Given the frequency of war, its influence over monetary affairs has been by no means uniform; rather what has mattered is a complex of forces, such as the fear of invasion, the duration of a war, its cost in money and lives, if it was fought domestically or overseas and whether its outbreak was motivated by civil unrest, conquest or defence.

Conflict from its outset can have an immediate impact on a nation's notes and coins and through more prolonged wars states find themselves needing to continue to react. The requirement to find a new equilibrium does not end with the drama of a few candle-burning sessions around the Cabinet table, or with the sleepless nights of a Prime Minister, and one of the thorniest of issues is how to pay for it all.

2 Financing war

Wars are not paid for in wartime, the bill comes later.

Benjamin Franklin

With combatants engaged, and any immediate currency crisis averted, states with any hope or prospect of successfully prosecuting a war have to be sure of their ability to find the necessary funds and sometimes at very short notice. Cardinal Richelieu, the seventeenth-century French statesman, summed up the requirement: 'Gold and money are among the chief and most necessary sources of the state's power...a poor prince would not be able to undertake glorious action.' Raising money through loans and taxes imposed on a population has been resorted to for centuries and their alignment with military objectives has been deliberate and understood. It probably comes as no great surprise that those states which became particularly effective at organising their financial and fiscal affairs have been amongst the foremost military powers. But, from time to time, less conventional methods have been employed.

Left. Groat of Henry VIII produced during the period of debasement, enlarged.

Finance through coinage

Henry VIII's debasement of gold and silver coins in the 1540s helped to finance war against France but it was not one of his more astute initiatives. Between 1544 and 1551, on a systematic basis, lower amounts of silver and gold were put into English coins than the currency-using public had come to expect. The financial success of the policy resulted in Henry and his son Edward VI (1547-53), who continued the debasement, profiting to the tune of about £1.25 million. Silver was attacked more aggressively than gold, with the historic sterling standard of 11oz 2dwt (925 fine) ultimately being reduced to 3oz (250 fine) and gold taken from 23 carats 3.5 grains (994.8 fine) progressively down to 20 carats (833 fine). It represented a hitherto unlooked for source of income for the crown but one that devastated the reputation of sterling for decades to come and it fell to Henry's daughter Elizabeth I (1558-1603) to re-build confidence in the currency.

Coinages have been subject to reductions in their precious metal content for centuries (Chapter 5, pp. 84-5) but to debase a coinage without any public announcement was to commit a cardinal fraud because it eroded that most important quality of a currency - trust. What made the situation an even greater shock was that the fineness of England's coinage had been maintained while many on the continent succumbed. During the Hundred Years War of the fourteenth and fifteenth centuries the French coinage was continually debased, contrasting sharply with the preservation of the 925 standard of English silver.

Of a different character, but still making use of the substance of the coinage to support the funding of a war, was the issue of base metal gun money in the late seventeenth century. Officially sanctioned copper farthing tokens had been produced in England earlier in the century but even when regal copper coins were introduced in the 1670s they remained very much second-class

Above. Gun money coins ranging
from a sixpence to thirty pence.

citizens of the currency system. So, for coins made principally of
copper to be employed as a form of wartime finance some twenty
years later in Ireland was a miraculous transformation.

James II (1685-8) had been forced out of England by William of
Orange in 1688 and having fled to France was persuaded his best
chance of returning to power lay in using southern Ireland as a
base. Battles needed to be fought against forces loyal to William
but gold and silver coins were in short supply in Dublin and the
idea was seized upon of producing coins from copper-based alloys.
More, though, than just providing a means of paying soldiers, the
coins bore an inscription which included, unusually, not only the
year but also the month of manufacture. The proposition was,
upon James regaining the throne, these base-metal pieces would
be redeemed in sequence in silver or gold. In this way the crowns,
half-crowns, shillings and sixpences of the series were given a

promissory status that came to be associated more readily with banknotes, and denominations were applied far above the intrinsic value of the metal they contained. More remarkable still was that their manufacture apparently included use of armaments, such as cannons and guns, as well as all manner of scrap brass and bronze in other forms, which accounts for the term gun money being applied some years later. This may well have been broken ordnance but, if serviceable weapons were being melted down, the enterprise presented the exquisite dilemma of producing an emergency coinage to fund a war, the supply of which gave precedence to paying soldiers over arming them.

The series included the striking of coins in the name of James II in the besieged town of Limerick, which followed on from the siege pieces produced fifty years earlier in a number of royalist towns blockaded by parliamentary forces (Chapter 3, p. 50). Between 1689 and 1691 the battles and sieges were ultimately won by William, with James escaping back to France, leaving those holding the next-to-worthless gun money with a promise never fully paid. Their use as small change may well have been tolerated for a time, but many were likely to have been discarded. A similar episode occurred in Russia in 1655 when Czar Alexis Mikhailovich, finding himself in financial difficulties as a result of war, resorted to issuing copper coins of the same size and value as the silver. It proved no more successful than the Irish and both are intriguing affairs since they inverted contemporary currency conventions through the elevation of base-metal coinages far above accepted levels.

Above. Engraving of the Bank of England dating from the 1730s. (© Governor and Company of the Bank of England.)

Financial and fiscal power

More legitimate ways in which to clothe, feed, equip and above all pay an army have included customs duties at ports, local and national taxes, stealing assets from a defeated opponent and simply asking supporters for cash. Duties were placed on beer, wine and tobacco for the first time in 1643 to raise money during the English Civil War, measures both sides claimed would be abolished after

the emergency requirement had passed. As is well known, however, they remain firmly embedded in the British tax system to this day. Then there was borrowing and from the late seventeenth century the ability of states to do this on a large scale was increasingly accessible. Banks had been open for business across Europe, with varying degrees of success, for many centuries and instances of public debt can be traced back to twelfth-century Venice. But the creation of a central bank, acting as lender of last resort to a government, changed the way in which a state could finance its activities. Operating with this brief the Bank of England, established in 1694, was something new and the timing directly related to William III's need to fund his campaigns against Louis XIV.

In the setting of enhanced expenditure on conflict in the late seventeenth century, the presence of the Bank of England provided a useful mechanism through which government could borrow to meet its commitments. Arising out of the extension of the Bank's influence, the money market in London developed more sophisticated financial instruments and the sector as a whole gradually assumed a distinct and powerful presence in the economy. By 1781 it was possible for the Prime Minister Lord North to describe the Bank as 'part of the constitution' and for the economist Adam Smith to refer to it as 'a great engine of state'.

Having an apparatus of government finance necessarily required a means through which to fund the debt and in England the state increasingly, and successfully, developed the ability to invent taxes, backed by a parliamentary system of scrutiny that provided legitimacy for such policies. A significant moment in the evolution of the British system of taxation came with the introduction of income tax for the first time in 1799 which was specifically designed as a war tax. Underpinning this was a reasonably efficient body of disinterested and salaried administrators devoted to collecting taxes. It was a form of bureaucracy that operated more efficiently than was the case on the continent, where the greater independence granted to tax collecting officials, for example in

France, harboured the potential for corruption. It was by no means perfect, nor without its pocket-lining practices, but it proved to be reliable and consequently generated its own standards and culture of probity. Of those working for government, a sizeable number came to be engaged in securing tax revenues and organising military activities. The combination of a more innovative money market and a sound fiscal base made a difference, and fed confidence in the whole mechanism of state finance.

Below. A group of tally sticks dating from the first half of the nineteenth century. They were used from medieval times to record payments into and out of the Exchequer, including taxes and fines.

During the eighteenth century Britain found itself drawn into conflicts more frequently than had been the case in the previous two centuries. As a nation it might have realised the financial means were now at its disposal with which to engage in wars and it was therefore more inclined to do so, maturing as a military state with commercially expansionist ambitions. From the Glorious Revolution of 1688-9 a number of elements had therefore come together, including the creation of a central bank, the development of a salaried tax-gathering bureaucracy, the presence of parliamentary institutions to help legitimise raising taxes and the growth of a national debt. Britain succeeded in operating these elements in concert more effectively than her European neighbours and was consequently able to realise their potential. Backed by such developments, Britain's status in Europe advanced during the course of the eighteenth century such that by 1815, and Wellington's victory at the Battle of Waterloo, it had become the dominant power. It was a position achieved with the help of its allies on the battlefield but Britain's ability to finance war meant it had not only funded its own forces but also bankrolled those of other major European powers ranged against Napoleon (1803-15).

Looking at Britain's currency over the same period reveals a somewhat delinquent monetary policy that generated severe shortages of silver and copper coins, particularly towards the end of the eighteenth century. But where the politicians of the age were right, whether by luck or judgement, was in placing their faith in gold and protecting that particular element of the money supply. As it transpired, the onward progress of Britain as a trading power, combined with the beginnings of the industrial revolution, made the support given to gold an ever more sensible approach.

Paying for war outstripped any other aspect of government expenditure by some distance for 250 years from the end of the seventeenth century and during this period it grew in importance as a public finance commitment. In Britain between the 1680s and

Above. Silver coins in circulation during the eighteenth century became excessively worn because of the increasing shortage of new coins.

1813, military expenditure fluctuated between 55% and 90% of total government spending. The average for the next hundred years was 34% but at its peak, in 1917, rose to 90% and a similarly high level of 84% was recorded in 1944. It was not until the advent of the much greater focus on welfare after the Second World War that the largest single element of government spending in Britain, as in many other Western countries, ceased to be defence.

Use and misuse of paper money

In a world where the banking sector became progressively more influential, its note issues came to occupy a larger proportion of the money supply and therefore played a more material part in currency arrangements when it came to funding military campaigns. Pressure to finance a war, though, led on more than one occasion to misjudgements of a catastrophic nature in how much paper money should be printed.

Use of bullion as currency necessarily comes with a built-in restraint mechanism generated by the simple reality of a limited supply of precious metal. Shorn of this control, at times the sound judgement of finance ministers foundered. One of the most extreme instances of this occurred during the French Revolutionary Wars when the National Assembly in Paris colluded in a massive over-issue of its

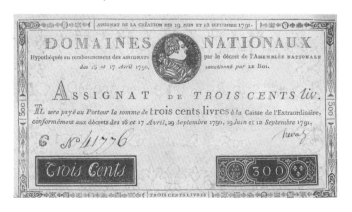

Left. An example of an assignat note issued under the authority of the French revolutionary government. (Courtesy of Spink.)

Bank-Notes,—Paper-Money,—French-Alarmists,—o, the Devil, the Devil!—ah! poor John-Bull!!!

assignat notes. In 1789 they were originally interest bearing and were used to fund the new government but from 1790 this stopped and by October 1792 the number in circulation had risen to over two billion. Their value decreased and they became a discredited form of currency, helping to generate unhealthy increases in inflation. Between 1789 and 1796 forty billion were eventually put into circulation and, from a convenient instrument of war finance, they came to undermine the legitimacy and stability of the revolutionary government. The lesson was learned by those involved and into the mid-nineteenth century France was still inclined to use coinage for transactions to a much greater extent than was the case in Britain.

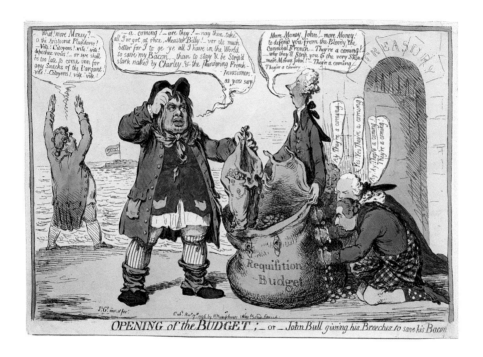

OPENING of the BUDGET; — or — John Bull giving his Breeches to save his Bacon

During the same conflict, freeing up reserves of gold to prosecute the war through a more extensive use of paper was no less important for Britain. If it managed matters a little better it was still not spared the scathing attentions of the satirists. Cartoonist James Gillray savaged politicians of the age with depictions of them hoarding gold and giving out what were referred to as worthless bank rags in their place. In one cartoon the hapless John Bull found himself being bamboozled by Prime Minister William Pitt, in the role of a bank teller, while opposition Whig MPs Charles Fox and Richard Sheridan urge him to decline the banknotes being offered and insist on guineas. In another Gillray cartoon the advent of higher rates of tax from 1796 led him to show John Bull giving up his trousers as his contribution.

Above. Higher taxes announced in the budget of 1796 had been stimulated by the ongoing conflict with France. James Gillray depicts an impoverished John Bull unable to pay his way. (© Governor and Company of the Bank of England.)

Below. A Confederate banknote for 500 dollars dating from 1864 issued in Richmond, Virginia. (Courtesy of Spink.)

Right. War loan bearer bonds issued by the British government during the First World War. (© Governor and Company of the Bank of England.)

The experience of excessive note issues during the American War of Independence (1775-83) generated a certain mistrust of currency in the form of paper but by the time of the American Civil War in the 1860s the memory seems to have faded. Taxes were used in the northern and southern states but in the south the fiscal measures were not sufficient to cover the costs of the conflict. The borrowing policy of the newly established Confederate government proved more successful than its ability to raise revenue through taxation but was still not enough and it proved necessary to resort to the printing press to fill the gap. Banknotes were produced under the authority of the Confederacy to fund its fight, being used to pay soldiers and provision the war effort. Although beautifully designed and released in a dizzying variety of types across many states, they decreased in value as a consequence of too many being printed, resulting in rapid inflation. When the conflict was over, Confederate notes were not recognised as currency by the victorious United States government and many were left with worthless works of currency art.

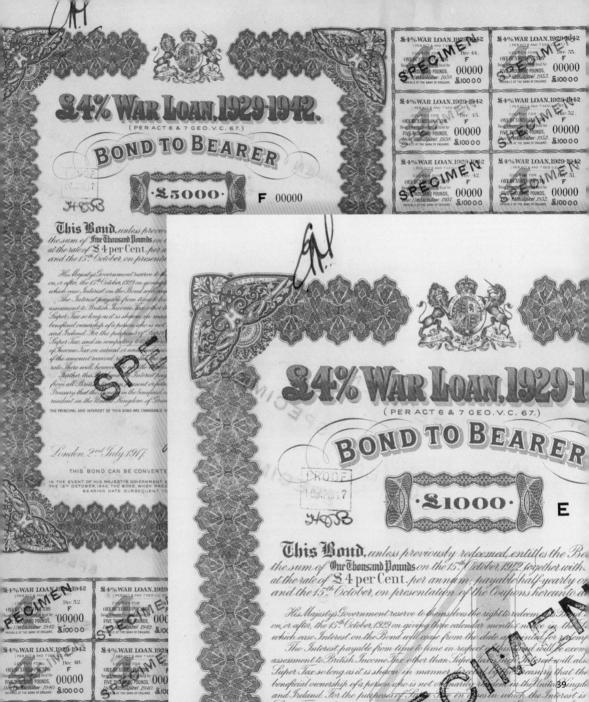

£4% War Loan, 1929-1942.
(PER ACT 6 & 7 GEO.V.C. 67.)

BOND TO BEARER

· £5000 ·   F   00000

This Bond, unless previously redeemed, entitles the Bearer to
the sum of Five Thousand Pounds on...
at the rate of £4 per Cent. per annum...
and the 15th October, on presentation...

His Majesty's Government reserve to...
on, or after, the 15th October, 1929 on giving three...
which case Interest on the Bond will cease...

The Interest payable from time to time...
assessment to British Income Tax other than...
Super Tax so long as it is shown in manner...
beneficial ownership of a person who is not...
and Ireland. For the purposes of Super Tax...
Super Tax, and in compiling...
of Income Tax on earned or unearned...
if the amount received...
rate. There will, however...
Further, this...Interest pay...
from all British...
Treasury that the...in the beneficial...
resident in the United Kingdom of Great...

THE PRINCIPAL AND INTEREST OF THIS BOND ARE CHANGEABLE O...

London, 2nd July 1917.

THIS BOND CAN BE CONVERTE...

IN THE EVENT OF HIS MAJESTY'S GOVERNMENT E...
THE 15TH OCTOBER, 1942. THE BOND, WHEN PRES...
BEARING DATE SUBSEQUENT TO...

£4% War Loan, 1929-1942.
(PER ACT 6 & 7 GEO.V.C. 67.)

BOND TO BEARER

· £1000 ·   E

This Bond, unless previously redeemed, entitles the Bea...
the sum of One Thousand Pounds on the 15th October 1942, together with...
at the rate of £4 per Cent. per annum, payable half yearly on...
and the 15th October, on presentation of the Coupons hereunto a...

His Majesty's Government reserve to themselves the right to redeem...
on, or after, the 15th October, 1929 on giving three calendar months' notice in the...
which case Interest on the Bond will cease from the date ap...entitled for redemp...

The Interest payable from time to time in respect of this Bond will be exem...
assessment to British Income Tax other than Super Tax such Interest will als...
Super Tax so long as it is shown in manner...that the...
beneficial ownership of a person who is not ordinarily resident in the United Kingdo...
and Ireland. For the purposes of Super Tax in the Interest is...
Super Tax, and in compiling total income for...purposes of Exemption, Abate...

39

IF EVERYBODY HELPED —

Above. As in the Napoleonic Wars, satirical cartoonists during the First World War were attracted by the theme of war and money, here on the side of the government in promoting war loans. (© Punch Ltd.)

A conflict of the scale and duration of the First World War required every ounce of money-raising ingenuity, new initiatives sitting alongside tried and trusted approaches. The government in Britain, as elsewhere, sought to fund military activity through the tax system and as soon as the war began the income tax rate doubled to 7.5%. By 1918 the rate was 30%. Taxes on excess profits were introduced and indirect taxation was also used, with hats and tickets to the cinema included. In France there was a substantial increase in note issues and it was not alone in using currency inflation as a means of meeting the costs of paying suppliers, financing industry and staving off public panic. But between 1913 and 1918 the expansion of paper currency in Germany was much greater and a not dissimilar surge was witnessed in Austria-Hungary, Russia and Britain. Across the belligerent nations emergency measures founded on suspending convertibility of notes into gold and borrowing heavily from central banks, especially in the first few months, enabled them to prosecute the war reasonably unrestrained. But the insatiable demand for cash placed a substantial burden on the banking sector. At a meeting in the City of London in July 1915 Reginald McKenna, Chancellor of the Exchequer between May 1915 and December 1916, put the cost of war at £3 million a day and the bankers in the room were left in no doubt of their obligation to help in any way they could. But the immense levels of expenditure required a material change to the way the state borrowed and, as with other aspects of the war, the mass of the population was called upon to become involved as never before.

Government bonds were sold on a large scale direct to the public by subscription, the language used in how they were promoted conveying messages of patriotism and duty to one's country. Films were commissioned to coax cash out of investors showing the munitions it would be possible to buy for standard subscription rates and highly emotive posters were printed in Austria-Hungary,

Germany, France and Britain on which coins often featured. They turned into bullets, assumed the proportion of tombstone-like weights to crush the enemy or were re-imagined as medieval shields. McKenna whilst Chancellor employed Hedley Le Bas of the Caxton Advertising Agency, who had been largely responsible for Lord Kitchener's recruitment campaign, to popularise the terms of the government's war loans. Through his work on promoting War Saving Certificates, Le Bas created some of the most memorable posters of the war, at one point commenting 'why not make patriotism profitable?'.

Longer-term, or perpetual loans, were an effective part of the initiative and in 1932 Neville Chamberlain as Chancellor converted the 1917 war loan, originally payable in 1947, into perpetual bonds paying 3.5%. As a result nearly £2 billion of war bonds remain in circulation to this day, giving ample validity to the reflections of Benjamin Franklin: 'Wars are not paid for in wartime, the bill comes later.' There was, however, also a requirement for short-term loans of only a few years in the form of Treasury bills, which in effect became monetised as central banks discounted them.

The same mix of borrowing facilities was accessed by governments in the Second World War and particularly amongst Axis Powers there was a reliance on short-term borrowing. In Germany and Italy wartime monetary growth reached seven or eight fold what it had been before the war, often the notes in question being short-term debt instruments bearing interest but their use had much the same impact on inflation as cash. In Britain more focus was placed on medium and longer-term loans and, by comparison, the overall money supply grew by less than a factor of three.

While gold may no longer have played a part in the daily routine of buying and selling, it still had a role in supporting the value of major currencies and its position during the Second World War,

LEND YOUR
FIVE SHILLINGS
TO YOUR COUNTRY
AND

CRUSH
THE GERMANS

Above. Highly emotive posters of the First World War encouraged mass participation in funding military activity.

therefore, weighed heavily on the minds of politicians and bankers. Extraordinary efforts were expended on arranging for reserves from several European countries to be shipped across the Atlantic under the ever-present threat of U-boat attacks. By keeping both gold and securities from falling into enemy hands the Allies hoped to continue to fund the war even in the event of invasion. Known as Operation Fish, in the first six months up to the beginning of 1940 Britain transported over 100 tonnes of gold to Canada for safe keeping. Given the number of ships lost at the time to enemy action, it was a considerable achievement that all the convoys arrived safely. Using converted passenger liners accompanied by naval convoys, by the end of the operation just over £500 million of gold at 1940s values had been shipped, amounting to a staggeringly large physical transfer of wealth from one nation to another. After the war this particular hoard of gold and securities found its way back to its owners by means of another highly secret and potentially hazardous Atlantic crossing.

The financing of war has left its imprint across many centuries and its impact on the substance of currencies has been no less telling. Whether Thomas Jefferson's assertion that banking institutions are more dangerous than standing armies has any validity is a debatable point but the borders between government debt and readily exchangeable money have at times become blurred, influencing the sense and reality of how much cash has been available at any one time. The introduction of particular notes and coins, too, such as gun money and Bradbury Treasury notes, have their origin in forbidding wartime circumstances characterised by pressing financial needs. There are, in addition, other instances of forms of money being created, sometimes specifically for armies, or of existing coins and notes being made in larger quantities stimulated by increased levels of economic activity and higher prices that arise as a consequence of war.

My cargo is only gold – nothing else.

Captain Klaas de Jong

We got sick to death of the sight of bullion.

Executive Officer, HMS *Emerald*

Hope you won't mind us dropping in unexpectedly like this, but we've brought along a large consignment of 'fish'.

Alexander Craig, Bank of England

Stadt-
Sparkaſſe
Bielefeld
500000

FÜNFHUNDERTTAUSEND MARK

Zahle gegen dieſen Scheck an uns
oder Ueberbringer aus Guthaben
Bielefeld, den 20.8.23. Der Magiſtrat

DRUCK: C.GUNDLACH A·G. BIELEFELD.

3 War and the creation of money

Ring out the narrowing lust of gold;
Ring out the thousand wars of old.

Alfred Lord Tennyson

From 1914 large tracts of the population of young men right across Europe acknowledged that their country needed them and accepted the call to join the ranks alongside the more modest numbers of professional soldiers. In France and Germany more than 13% of the population mobilised, whereas in Britain the figure was about 9%. Such mass participation contrasts with the centuries-old system of mercenary forces, not infrequently drawn from several countries, the common loyalty binding them together being money. The requirement to pay an army stimulated demand for additional amounts of cash, over and above that in normal circulation, and in some cases to meet the need new types of currency were created.

For military use

In most instances coins otherwise destined for everyday transactions would be re-directed to cover supplies and soldiers' pay but from time to time special arrangements were made and

Left. German municipal notes issued during the First World War from Bielefeld and Eisenach. (Courtesy of Spink.)

Above. Wellington painted by
Francisco de Goya, 1812-4.
(© National Portrait Gallery, London.)

occasionally it is possible to identify the specific coins, or elements of production, struck for war. When the Earl of Leicester embarked on a campaign in the Netherlands in 1585 he took with him 18,000 fine gold coins specially struck for the purpose at a time when large quantities of such gold pieces were not generally in production.

During the Peninsular War (1808-14) there were problems with supplying the army right from the start. Responsibility for furnishing its requirements rested with the Commissariat which from its origins had been controlled by the Treasury, an arrangement sustained well into the nineteenth century. The reality on the ground was that although John Herries, the Commissary-in-Chief, controlled the Treasury's officials abroad he acted in close cooperation with the commander of British forces, Wellington, and both were required to address an increasingly urgent absence of hard currency.

The French system was to live off the country, to pay for nothing and to aim to make a profit out of a campaign, whereas the British approach was to pay for everything, partly in the hope of winning hearts and minds along the way, and to support the troops with convoys of supplies. Herries noted that the French boasted of being able to maintain four men in the Peninsula for the cost of one British soldier, 'the difference is of course made up by robbery'. If Shakespeare was recording anything like the reality of military operations in the early fifteenth century in *Henry V*, it seems to have been an English tradition for some time.

> Henry V: We would have all such offenders so cut off:
> and we give express charge, that in our marches through
> the country, there be nothing compelled from the
> villages, nothing taken but paid for, none of the
> French upbraided or abused in disdainful language;
> for when lenity and cruelty play for a kingdom, the
> gentler gamester is the soonest winner.

Wellington has been described as 'a prince of grumblers' and he certainly complained regularly of being constrained in his ability to operate because of lack of money. His woes, conveyed through despatches, were numerous but at times he had a point, being hindered by how the Treasury itself acquired currency on the continent through its network of agents. Some, like Andrew Cochrane Johnstone, were thoroughly disreputable characters, largely in the employ of the state to further their own interests.

The need for a currency that could be used locally in the Peninsula took the form of Spanish dollars but as these ran dry bills of exchange came to be used more frequently. Nevertheless, this widely accepted silver coin continued to have a key role to play. Spencer Perceval,

Below. Artwork by Harry Eccleston for the Bank of England Series D five-pound note, first issued in 1973, showing Wellington in action during the Peninsular War. (© Governor and Company of the Bank of England.)

Above. Spanish dollars of this type circulated widely and were essential in funding the British war effort against Napoleon in Spain. (Courtesy of Morton & Eden.)

first as Chancellor of the Exchequer and then as Prime Minister, devoted a considerable amount of energy to seeking out quantities of silver dollars to send out to Wellington for use by British forces and in support of Spanish insurgents. In March 1808 the merchant Sir Francis Baring obtained 1,500,000 dollars from Mexico and the reserves of the silver coin held by the Bank of England were called upon as well. By the summer of 1809 the army's financial position had become critical. Payments to local suppliers and soldiers often ran months in arrears. Wellington calculated that the army needed £200,000 a month to meet all its commitments and in June of that year he remarked 'we are over head and ears in debt everywhere', criticising the army's commissaries of being 'incompetent to a man'. Amongst other amounts of dollars, Perceval managed to secure 500,000 in February 1810 which were shipped to Portugal on the *Comus*. In April the Treasury obtained 63,573 dollars from a source in Jamaica, bought a further 400,000 from the Bank of England and an additional 600,000 arrived from Argentina in June. Perceval urged the Bank to buy up all the dollars it could that were imported into Britain but inevitably some went to merchants.

A great deal more specie was raised in the Peninsula during the following year and Wellington for once seemed less critical of the politicians and officials back in London. But shortages re-emerged in 1812. He estimated that the British army was in debt to the tune of 5,000,000 dollars and pay to the troops was again months overdue. He made efforts himself to obtain a quantity of dollars in March from Gibraltar, his personal interest in these transactions being motivated by a concern to ensure the forces under his command were paid regularly to avoid indiscipline through instances of looting in local areas. The strength of his feeling against soldiers plundering led to his imposing the penalty of immediate hanging. 'Our own troops will always fight', he wrote, 'but the influence of regular pay is seriously felt on their conduct, their health, and their efficiency'. The search for sufficient quantities of dollars remained a running sore throughout the greater part of the war and the costs of finding the vast amounts needed challenged Perceval's ministry on more than one occasion.

Gold coins also played a part. With the exception of 1797 and 1798, gold had not been minted in Britain in any substantial amount since the early 1790s but an exception was made towards the end of the war. The coins, dated 1813, which came to be known as military guineas, were shipped out to Wellington for use in the Peninsula. Only about 360,000 were produced, making them one of the smaller mintages of guineas and, as matters transpired, they were the last to be produced. In 1814 the Treasury gave the banker Nathan Rothschild a secret commission to purchase specie on its behalf and the difficulties over ready cash seemed from that time to have faded away. Herries worked closely with Rothschild and both proved successful in finding quantities of bullion. Some years later Herries was appointed Master of the Mint and attracted the praise of Prime Minister William Gladstone, who remembered him as a particularly able administrator.

Above. Military guinea dated 1813.

Below. Louis d'Or gold coins were made at the Mint on Tower Hill for use by British troops in France.

Paying for campaigns by using foreign currency extended beyond the Spanish dollar and involved at times actually making the money of other states. From 1813 the Mint in London had been busy striking Hanoverian gold five-thaler pieces for the army although, with George III being the King of Hanover, such production strictly speaking did not amount to making another country's coinage. Production of French Louis d'Or twenty franc gold coins in 1815, however, was a different matter. The purpose in mind was to supply British troops in France with coins they could readily spend. In sanctioning the activity the government in Westminster stressed it was acting with the approval of the exiled Louis XVIII. The local French authorities took a different view. They objected, claiming the coins had not been made to the correct standard, a slur officials in London strongly disputed but, unlike many other instances of one state producing the money of another during a war, here Britain was not seeking to use coinage as an instrument of disruption.

Above. Vienna six kreuzer siege piece of 1529. (Courtesy of John Porteous.)

Right. Siege pieces were produced in Magdeburg during the Thirty Years War (top – courtesy of John Porteous) and in several towns during the English Civil War, including Pontefract (bottom), enlarged.

The requirement for a foreign army to use a currency well-known locally, as Wellington found with Spanish dollars, is entirely understandable and consequently is encountered elsewhere. Maria Theresa thalers proved an essential element of the British military expedition in 1867 to rescue the British Consul Charles Duncan Cameron, and other European nationals, who had been taken hostage by Emperor Theodore of Ethiopia (1855-68). A senior figure in the undertaking wrote of the expedition in his official report that 'it was found absolutely necessary to have a supply of thalers with the leading columns, so as to pay at once for supplies tendered and establish a feeling of confidence in the country'. Consequently, the expedition needed to find as many as possible and at one point the mint in Vienna was asked to supply some directly to the expedition, shipping them out from Trieste through Alexandria to Suez and on to the Red Sea.

Creation of money locally

Another category of war currency materialised locally in conditions where groups found themselves cut off from normal sources of supply. Advances in siege warfare during the sixteenth and seventeenth centuries made it a more effective tactic and cities with an army camped outside the gates sometimes chose to create their own emergency money. There are early examples from Vienna when, besieged by the Turks in 1529, crudely shaped gold and silver coins were produced. About a hundred years later the city of Breda in the Netherlands, blockaded by Spanish forces, generated silver twenty sous pieces of similarly exotic shapes. Then during the 1640s royalist strongholds in England found themselves needing to pay garrisons to ensure their continued commitment. At Newark, Scarborough, Carlisle and Pontefract improvised money was produced and, like some of the earlier examples, the rough-hewn shapes were a consequence of the source material being cut up pieces of domestic silverware. Carlisle became an isolated royalist outpost in the north of England when the city was besieged by a Scots army from October 1644. Every citizen, it is recorded, was ordered to offer up their silver plate to be coined and in May 1645 one and three-shilling pieces were the outcome.

Notes, too, have been produced under such conditions, like those issued during the siege of Mafeking, South Africa, in 1900 during the Boer War which carried designs created by Baden Powell, who later founded the scouting movement. Even more focused in their use were the currencies of necessity conceived in internment camps during the Second World War, such as those on the Isle of Man. Brass tokens for halfpennies, pennies and sixpences were made and employed as currency in the Onchan camp bearing a denominational value on one side and the distinctive Manx three-legged symbol on the other. In a not dissimilar way cigarettes came to be treated as a medium of exchange in a more purely military setting, with soldiers separated from an adequate supply of regular currency turning to one of the most widely accepted commodities.

Beyond the confines of a besieged city or barbed wire camp, local communities found solutions for shortages of money when necessity pressed. The great scarcity of small change in a number of countries at the beginning of the First World War led to a localised use of

Right. Paper currency designed and produced during the siege of Mafeking in 1900. (Courtesy of Spink.)

postage stamps as currency, including in Russia, where stamp designs were specially adapted for the purpose. There were sizeable increases in the amount of currency circulating in Germany during the early months of the war, taking the form of Treasury bills and notes issued by loan banks. But there were still shortages of cash arising from individuals hoarding coinage and the pressures of mobilisation. When the state could not cope, regional centres took matters into their own hands, resulting in the creation of a prodigious array of currencies. Private credit backed the issue in Germany of emergency money struck or printed by chambers of commerce and municipal bodies, mines and manufacturers. The Prince of Pless owned mines near Waldenburg and from October 1914, without access to regular money markets, his agents took to paying workers in notes backed by his own personal credit for denominations ranging from one to ten marks. There were instances of torn pieces of paper embossed with the rubber stamp of the town concerned noting it was 'Good for 2M', or of cardboard notes being issued by grocers, some purely descriptive of their function but others quite attractively conceived. In Belgium local coinages were created in Ghent and in the commune of Rouveroy, to name but two amongst many, and subsidiary currencies were issued throughout France in a range of metals, such as brass and zinc in La Rochelle

Left. A note denominated half a crown used in the Onchan internment camp on the Isle of Man during the Second World War. (Courtesy of Spink.)

Above and below. The vast majority of currency used during the English Civil War was produced by the Mint in the Tower, such as sixpences (above) and half-crowns (below).

and aluminium in Carcassonne and Le Havre. In their highly localised nature they are reminiscent of the token issues of late eighteenth-century England, a failure of the state to address the requirements of demand for money in both instances lying at the heart of the matter.

Output and the incidence of war

Money, therefore, can take many forms in the setting of war but regular definitive issues usually bear the greater burden. The amounts made have varied substantially, both rising and falling, in response to unrest as can be seen by tracking production levels at the Royal Mint during major conflicts over an extended period of time.

Starting in the seventeenth century, the English Civil War reveals a marked increase in output. The number of silver coins produced was on a rising trend during the early seventeenth century thanks to the availability of Spanish silver but for most of the 1640s output was higher than in the decades immediately preceding and after, with a noticeable spike evident just before the war started. It is thought the prospect of conflict brought about a strong desire on the part of government and others to turn silver into coin and the upward trend continued over the next three years.

Those arranging the logistics of finding enough money to pay the wages of soldiers at this time encountered difficulties. One issue lay in the rates of pay offered to troops being higher than might otherwise be expected, as suggested by the royalist Earl of Northampton paying two shillings a day to lay siege to Warwick Castle in 1642 when normally the cost of labour might be no more than a few pence. A more standard and lower rate settled on by both sides in the conflict was eight pence a day given to infantrymen with more offered to the cavalry. Finding sufficient amounts to pay these higher wages was itself an issue but a paymaster's troubles were exacerbated by large-scale hoarding which reduced the stock of available coins further still (Chapter 4, pp. 62-4). While output of coins therefore might have increased during the war, the supply of currency looks to have struggled to keep pace with the demands being placed upon it.

Increases in levels of Mint output have come about for a number of reasons and in many instances have been the consequence of planned recoinages or routine currency husbandry. As previously noted (Chapter 1, p. 23), the increase in silver production in the 1690s was massively skewed by the Great Recoinage which can itself be linked to war between England and France. But the large increase in the number of guineas being minted in the mid 1770s was a consequence of the need to renew the condition of coins in domestic circulation and had little connection with Britain's fight across the Atlantic during the early stages of the American War of Independence.

Output of English gold and silver coins, 1630–1700

Gold   Silver

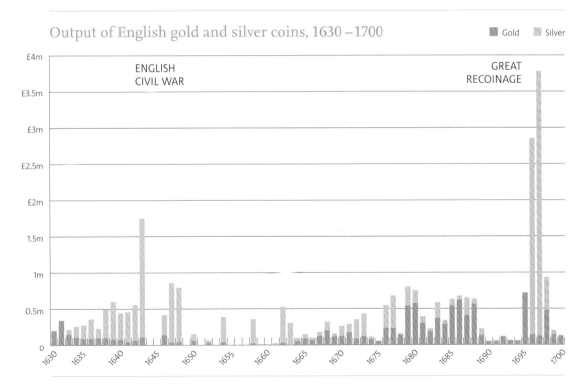

War between Britain and France from the 1790s was registered in output changes of gold in the direction of a noticeable decline as a result of the restrictions placed on cash payments. The exception to this lower level came from 1811 when production started of silver tokens issued under the authority of the Bank of England. It was a wartime expedient in the form of two pieces given unusual face values, one of three shillings and the other eighteen pence, to avoid a clash with the existing range of coins. They were made in significant numbers and provided a much-needed boost to the silver circulation which had been starved of supply for decades even before the war. Towards the end of the nineteenth century, large amounts of silver were produced for use in South Africa during the Boer War which was reflected in a noticeable rise in production. The advent of the First World War, too, saw an advance in output of silver and bronze coins. In 1916 production of silver reached over £8 million for the first time in one year and two years later it was over £9 million.

Output of bronze experienced a marked uplift from 1916 and was sustained at an elevated level throughout the war. Gold was still being produced in 1915-6 but in declining amounts and the increase in production of other alloys was a reflection of the system re-adjusting itself. Even with the decline in output of gold from the vast pre-war levels, the overall amount of coin being struck by the Mint increased, supplemented by those required for British colonies.

In the Second World War there was a marked change in output. The first years saw the rate of production of silver double from the pre-war levels, increasing to £10.6 million in 1942 and being sustained above pre-war rates in subsequent years. For bronze the output, if anything, fell but from 1937 it had been sharing the lower denomination territory with the nickel-brass threepence and output of these coins increased, reaching a peak of £1.2 million in 1942-3. It is thought their popularity was influenced by their shape, the ease of recognising the distinctive twelve sides being especially appreciated during blackouts.

Money, then, has been called into being in specific forms because of conflict to address the requirements of those carrying the guns but also to meet the needs of the population at large during periods of increased economic activity or disruption to the normal channels of supply. Arms and armour cost, and fortunes made on the back of wars have been frequently noted. On returning to the House of Commons after the First World War, the Conservative politician Stanley Baldwin observed the chamber to be populated by 'a lot of hard-faced men who look as if they had done very well out of the war'. Less expected are the changes that can take place in how coins and banknotes are used and the way in which they are physically transformed. Wars witness behavioural shifts in relation to currency, often emotionally driven but, in addition, sometimes currencies themselves become combatants and active players in the theatre of conflict.

Above. Twelve-sided threepence produced during the Second World War.

4 An ornament and a safeguard

The money that we possess is the instrument of liberty.

Jean-Jacques Rousseau

Finding uses for money completely divorced from its function as currency has a rich and varied tradition. Roman coins were incorporated into pieces of jewellery and employing coins as weights for the clock mechanism of Big Ben or to gauge the height of a printer's block, as a marker for a golf ball on a putting green or as a plectrum for the guitarist Brian May are indicative of the alternative lives they have led.

Hoarding

In the absence of high-street banks, storing coins in hoards to make financial provision for the future was not uncommon. Hiding them in a safe location in response to an army appearing over the horizon was slightly different but was equally well-rehearsed. Through numerous periods of turmoil, from classical times to the twentieth century, the wealth of an individual, rich or poor, has been set aside to be retrieved at some future time when peace again prevails.

Left. Necklace of the late nineteenth century made up of Afghan and Indian coins. (Courtesy of Harry Mernick.)

Below. Gold coins from the reigns of James I (1603-25) and Charles I representing types likely to have been included in the hoard buried by Samuel Pepys in 1667, enlarged.

One of the better known accounts is provided by Samuel Pepys who, on 13th June 1667, fearing an imminent invasion as Dutch ships sailed up the Medway, had his wife and father bury about £1300 in gold coins at his country house in Brampton, Cambridgeshire. The account of the episode in his diary provides the kind of direct personal evidence which is more frequently lacking. At the time, through his role as Clerk of the Acts to the Navy Board, he was heavily involved in keeping the Navy supplied, which daily generated financial concerns, but he was also quite understandably at pains to secure the safety of his own property. Some days after instructing his wife to bury the coins he fell out with her on hearing how poorly she had hidden them in the garden of the house but it was not until 10th October that he set about digging them up.

My father and I, with a dark lantern; it being now night, into the garden with my wife, and there went about our great work to dig up my gold. But, Lord! what a tosse I was for some time in, that they could not justly tell where it was; that I begun heartily to sweat, and be angry, that they should not agree better upon the place, and at last to fear that it was gone but by and by poking with a spit, we found it, and then begun with a spudd to lift up the ground.

He had acted in very much the same way in response to the threatening advance of the Great Fire of London a year earlier but on that occasion he used his garden in London and thought to include his wine and parmesan cheese as well as his gold.

Lacking documentary sources of the type provided by Pepys means the link between a hoard being deposited and the purpose the depositor had in mind can only be recreated by investigating the contextual evidence. But by doing just that it is possible to build up a picture of the reasons involved and the outcome can rightly challenge thinking which too readily sees an answer in a threatening military situation. Particularly in Iron Age hoards, religious or ceremonial reasons emerge where the intention was not to retrieve the coins at all. Moreover, if not all hoards have been inspired by war, not all wars have inspired hoarding. There are periods of conflict which show little advance in the incidence of coins being deposited. No noticeable increase is apparent when the ships of the Spanish Armada circled off the coast of England in 1588 and, for all the panic of a French invasion in 1797, and the subsequent long war, the incidence of coins being laid down did not suddenly escalate. Nevertheless, a glance at the high points of hoarding from Anglo-Saxon times demonstrates an undeniable link with war. A peak is encountered during the Viking raids of the mid-ninth century, another advance between 1060 and 1070 coincides with the conquest of William I (1066-87) and the civil unrest of Stephen's reign between 1135 and 1154 sees a distinct rise.

Above. Painting of Samuel Pepys by John Hayls, 1666. (© National Portrait Gallery, London.)

It is by no means always the answer but there is a strong and justifiable connection between hoards and war, the underlying objective more often than not being to take back possession of the coins in question.

To focus on one period, the English Civil War represents the largest incidence of hoarding in post-Roman British history. An average of one hoard a year has been discovered and recorded for the reigns of James I and Charles II (1660-85), and this is also the case for the first twelve years of the reign of Charles I. By contrast, the decade from 1639 to 1649 has yielded at least 189 hoards with secure dates of deposit, with another 170 or more likely to have come from these years. With battles between royalists and parliamentarians being fought in many parts of the country, a pattern is apparent whereby gold and silver were hidden away in roof spaces, under floors, up chimneys as well as in the ground. The uncertainty of the time and the advent of a battle in the vicinity prompted many of these deposits but sometimes it might have been motivated by fear of the military force in question confiscating a family's accumulated wealth.

More than the plain reality of the number of instances, the size, composition, specific location and sometimes the likely owners can provide insights into how money was used and how wealth was distributed. In 1996 the hoard of 467 silver and thirty-three gold coins found at Tregwynt, not far from Fishguard in Pembrokeshire, is a case in point. It is one of the finest coin hoards ever found in Wales, containing coins from the first half of the seventeenth century but also pieces dating back to the sixteenth century, including a gold five-shilling crown of Henry VIII, as well as silver sixpences and shillings of Edward VI, Philip and Mary (1554-8), and Elizabeth I. Unusually, it also included coins from seven of the royalist mints in operation during the Civil War. The context of its burial almost certainly relates to the series of royalist risings in Wales during 1648, one of which centred on Pembrokeshire, and the presence of such a range of royalist coins suggests the owner may have been a supporter of Charles I. Tregwynt was occupied

at the time by the Harries family and there is some evidence to suggest they had royalist sympathies. The association cannot be proven conclusively but it offers the most plausible explanation. Linking specific hoards with particular moments in time and therefore individual battles can be problematic but, taking the period as a whole, where clusters of hoards occur at about the time a battle was fought, a reasonably persuasive case can often be made for such deposits reflecting military activity.

The absence of wars being fought within the borders of a given country will work to reduce the likelihood of hoards being laid down but even when battle is raging elsewhere anxiety arising from living through an unsettled period can influence behaviour. There are at least twelve hoards of gold coins deposited between 1912 and 1915, one of the largest from Wantage in Berkshire consisting of 264 coins buried around 1915. It probably relates to the hostilities of the First World War and might reflect a wish to conceal personal wealth from the authorities. Combined with others from the period, the First World War represented the most significant revival in hoarding for some considerable time.

As already mentioned, a hoard does not have to be buried in the ground. There are many other hiding places or, applied more generally, it could refer to the spiriting away of wealth. The actions of Emperor Haile Selassie (1930-74) following the invasion of Ethiopia by Benito Mussolini in 1935 might be seen in this light. Having fled the country the following year on the British cruiser HMS *Enterprise* it was discovered he had with him many thousands of Maria Theresa thalers packed away on board, the historic silver coin being an important part of the Ethiopian economy.

Survival and defence

While burying coins in a hole in the ground or hiding them up the chimney is deferring their use as money, it is not actually altering how a currency is regarded. There are, though, many instances in which the setting of war induces alternative uses for money. In Patrick O'Brian's historical novel *The far side of the world*, set during the Napoleonic Wars, the ship's surgeon, Dr Maturin, patches a skull-wound with a silver coin.

> It was an operation that Dr Maturin had carried out at sea before, always in the fullest possible light and therefore on deck, and many of them had seen him do so. Now they and all their mates saw him do it again: they saw Joe Plaice's scalp taken off, his skull bared, a disc of bone audibly sawn out, the handle turning solemnly; a three-shilling piece, hammered into a flattened dome by the armourer, screwed on over the hole; and the scalp replaced, neatly sewn up by the parson.

He goes on to observe that it was a gruesome sight but one 'not to be missed for a mint of money'. A three-shilling piece was an interesting coin for O'Brian to have chosen since, as noted earlier (Chapter 3, p. 56), it was something of a war-inspired issue and at 35mm was an appropriately large coin for the purpose.

In the story a coin saves the sailor's life by aiding in the mending of a serious wound but coins have played a more active role, quite literally in the line of fire. Several soldiers have lived to tell the tale of how a coin, strategically or luckily placed, has stopped or deflected the path of a bullet and in some cases the account can be verified by the survival not only of the soldier but of the coin in question. In Germany during war with France in the early seventeenth century an officer was said to have survived when a bullet struck a large silver coin bearing an image of St George and the dragon. The silver thaler of Mansfeld thereafter acquired something of a reputation as a talisman and there was significant demand for them, well above their face value, from soldiers fighting in the Thirty Years War of 1618-48.

There are examples, too, from the battle of Culloden in 1746 and from the Napoleonic Wars. In a newspaper article published in 2015 the effects of a soldier from the First World War, Ivanhoe Avon who served in the Royal Welsh Fusiliers, were reported as including two pennies, one Victorian, the other of Edward VII, both partly pierced. The story passed down through the family relayed how these coins saved his life in 1916 at the Battle of the Somme. He not only carried them for luck during the rest of the war but for the rest of his life.

Left. Canadian soldiers in the trenches near Willerval during the First World War, 1918. (© IWM.)

Top and above. Ivanhoe Avon (top) pictured in uniform during the First World War and (above) the two coins that saved his life. (Courtesy of Marion Avon.)

Personalising money

Of a much less dramatic nature, there are examples of coins playing an emotional as opposed to an economic role in the setting of war. It has been suggested that gold coins carried by sailors on the *Mary Rose* when it sank in the Solent in 1545 might have been regarded as a type of good luck charm. The presence of gold angels, which bore a fairly prominent image of St Michael lancing a serpent, may well have had greater use as religious pocket pieces than they would as money on a ship in the midst of a battle.

At the more decorative end of the spectrum, if lent a political edge, are the siege pieces of the English Civil War (Chapter 3, p. 50). They were usually sophisticated enough to be denominated but pierced examples survive suggesting they were worn as royalist badges in

Above. A sixpence siege piece of Newark pierced as if to be worn.

Below. Painting of the *Mary Rose* from the Anthony Roll, 1546. (© Pepys Library, Magdalene College, Cambridge.)

support of Charles I or his exiled son the future Charles II. Changing the physical appearance of money is encountered during the Great War with soldiers engraving personal messages on coins. Shell cases were a favoured medium but messages were carved into the surface of pennies, and other denominations, frequently to a wife or family member. Their crude appearance is suggestive of the basic tools available but there are instances of some being especially well thought-through, bearing designs inspired by regimental badges. Coins were also hollowed out to conceal a message which may have more relevance to the activities of spies than to a homesick infantryman. More often, though, souvenirs were being created of time spent on the front line, a personalised piece to handle and provide reassurance.

Above. A silver coin skillfully engraved with the design of the cap badge of the Royal Artillery and bearing the inscription 'From a friend to a friend'.

Another form of souvenir is to be found in relation to the Second Afghan War, 1878-80, from which soldiers returned home with necklaces and belts ornately populated with a range of coins of the region, including Afghan one and half rupees. It is thought such items were purchased at the time and brought home as mementos of the campaign. Souvenirs have also been created from coins stolen by soldiers during war. Victorious armies have long been associated with the sacking of territories, one of their prizes frequently being cash in whatever form it was readily to hand. The instances are countless, but one example is that of the British army during the Sudan War of the 1890s, known as the Mahdist War, stealing coins following the re-capture of Khartoum. On returning home, soldiers retained the Sudanese currency as souvenirs and a number found their way to the prominent silversmiths Sampson Mordan & Co who incorporated them into silver ashtrays.

After a battle is over, coins have come to play a part in acts of commemoration. There are now numerous modern collector coins performing this function (Chapter 6, pp. 106-9) and, linking with war memorials, a set of coins was included in the contents of the time capsule buried beneath the Women at War sculpture by John Mills in Westminster. As a personal touch, Mills was allowed to place a specimen of a D-Day Landings fifty pence piece in the casket, a coin he had designed some years earlier. A relatively recent practice has emerged of coins being left on the graves of United States servicemen. It is thought to be an act of remembrance on the part of another soldier, with differences in the denominations of coins having symbolic meaning. A nickel is supposed to represent two soldiers who trained together, while a quarter indicates having been present at the soldier's death.

Weapons of war

A coin acting as the last line of defence in saving a life is extraordinary but money has been employed in more belligerent ways, too, such as French francs being placed on railway lines during the Second World War to slow down or incapacitate trains.

Above. Original artwork by John Mills for the coin issued to commemorate the fiftieth anniversary of the D-Day landings in 1994.

Left. Silver ashtray with a Sudanese coin mounted at the centre and bearing an inscription indicating the origins of the coin, 'From the Khalifa's Treasure House Omdurman'. (Courtesy of Harry Mernick.)

Above and below. Detail of the figure of Britannia (above) from a counterfeit ten-pound note produced as part of Operation Bernhard and (below) the front of the same note. (© Governor and Company of the Bank of England.)

If not using coinage itself as a weapon, Ibrahim Pasha, a leading military figure in the Middle East during the first half of the nineteenth century, used it as an incentive in a fairly gruesome manner. Acting under the orders of the Ottoman Sultan, Ibrahim invaded central Arabia in 1816 with the objective of bringing down the Saudi family. As a form of encouragement he offered his soldiers five Maria Theresa thalers for every pair of enemy ears taken.

In a more systematic way, states have actively sought to weaken an enemy by using currency in the theatre of economic warfare. Counterfeiting at a governmental level or, to put it more gently, imitating the coinage of another territory, has centuries of tradition. Sometimes no harm was meant by it when directed at providing a means of furthering trade through the production of familiar types, such as copies of English silver coins, known as continental sterlings, emanating from the Low Countries in the first half of the fourteenth century. Germany, too, in the First World War during its occupation of western parts of Iran, produced excellent 'forgeries' of 1000 and 2000 dinar coins to facilitate war-related trade rather than to create economic disorder. Matters might be

regarded as having taken a more consciously hostile turn when, during the French Revolutionary Wars, Britain engaged in counterfeiting assignats. As it transpired the massive over-issue meant the series imploded in any case but Britain's intent was clear: in making and putting the counterfeits into circulation it was seeking to undermine the French currency and to de-stabilise its economy. The British state seems to have been quite keen on the approach since it had done the same thirty years earlier during the American War of Independence.

Above and below. Comparing the counterfeit on p. 72 with this genuine Bank of England ten-pound note reveals both the skill but also the elements omitted by the counterfeiters. (© Governor and Company of the Bank of England.)

One of the best known instances of a nation engaging money to its cause is that of Operation Bernhard during the Second World War. Germany embarked upon making quantities of Bank of England notes with the intention of dropping them over Britain to destroy faith in the economy and weaken sterling. In the early days of the programme's development Hitler was personally interested and his support looks to have provided the initial impetus. The operation began in 1942 and, rather than use German citizens, 140 prisoners in concentration camps were transferred to a specially built compound in Sachsenhausen camp, north of Berlin. Their backgrounds and skills were varied but included engravers and

73

Above. The story of Operation Bernhard was so compelling it was turned into a German film released originally in 2007 under the title *Die Fälscher* (The Counterfeiters). (©AF archive/Alamy stock photograph.)

draughtsmen from several nations, their task being to unravel the fiendishly complex layers of security embedded within the seemingly straightforward design of five, ten, twenty and fifty pound notes. They had to solve the numbering system, the engraving of the vignette of Britannia, match dates with signatures and arrive at the right type of paper bearing the correct type of ink. Eventually a professional counterfeiter was recruited, a Russian by the name of Salomon Smolianoff, known as Solly. Different categories of counterfeits were produced. The best were used for buying foreign exchange in neutral countries and providing expenses for German spies. Below this, and likely to be subject to less scrutiny, were those employed for bribing collaborators, while a third category was reserved for a potential air-drop over England to cause economic disruption.

In the region of twelve million notes, with a face value of £150 million, are thought to have been printed. Once the Bank of England detected the first counterfeits, notes issued above five pounds were cancelled and a programme of gradually withdrawing those released prior to the start of hostilities was put in place. As a front in the war it did not succeed in its desired objectives and the falling out amongst the senior German officials involved reveals a comic drama of internal scheming which at times undermined what they themselves were trying to achieve.

Seeking to disrupt the economy of an enemy through the militarisation of money might be seen to operate on one side of an equation, the other side of which could be judged offering financial support to a network of allies. One way this was done during the Second World War by Britain was parachuting sovereigns into Greece to help with its war effort. Still today the gold sovereign occupies a special place in the monetary affections of the Greek people, with the price of gold being quoted in local newspapers in relation to the coin rather than ounces. Perhaps the loyalty to the sovereign has been reinforced by the re-telling of stories of gold raining down from the sky many years before.

Such operations were part of a use of currency in the clandestine war against Germany that also involved British spies being given sovereigns as part of their routine kit. A generation earlier T. E. Lawrence, better known as Lawrence of Arabia, was given substantial numbers of sovereigns by the government which he used to ingratiate himself with local tribal leaders he encountered in the Middle East. Furnishing members of the intelligence service with gold coins is well enough recorded, and the same has applied to special forces into more recent times, but a previously undocumented instance in the Second World War is provided by Tangye Lean, brother of the famous film director David Lean. A London book seller purchased from his widow a long run of the scholarly periodical, *Annual of the British School at Athens*, which was primarily devoted to the archaeology of ancient Greece. In subsequently checking the volumes it was found three contained combinations of about twenty sovereigns or guineas taped in cellophane holders to the inside back covers. Tangye Lean had been a fairly well-known journalist and BBC broadcaster, and during the Second World War had worked for the Political Warfare Executive, an intelligence branch of the Foreign Office which operated to undermine enemy morale through various forms of propaganda. His widow was entirely unaware of the coins. Given the range of dates and types, they appear to have been somewhat randomly acquired from the London dealing community and were then handed out to British intelligence agents, like Tangye Lean.

Above. Tangye Lean, British journalist and intelligence agent during the Second World War, was given gold coins to help carry out his duties for the Foreign Office. (© National Portrait Gallery, London.)

Relatively small amounts of currency being used in creative ways by soldiers would, naturally, have no impact on overall stocks but wide-spread hoarding, as experienced during the English Civil War, probably did make a difference. As a result of such unfamiliar forces exerting pressure on the money supply, state mints and central bank printing presses have found themselves under added stress during times of unrest. Pressure in making currency has also come from insecurity attaching to supply chains. Sources of material, formerly taken for granted, dry up and how coins and notes come to be made in a time of conflict has necessitated creative solutions.

Mints operating during the reign of Stephen

◆ Locations at which coins were struck in the name of Stephen

● Locations at which coins were struck for Empress Matilda and the Barons, including irregular local issues

◈ Locations at which coins were struck for Stephen and Empress Matilda, including irregular types

Bamburgh

Corbridge

Carlisle

Newcastle

Durham

Richmond

York

Hedon

Chester

Lincoln

Nottingham

Stafford

Derby

Tutbury

Shrewsbury

Tamworth

Leicester

Stamford

Castle Rising

Norwich

Warwick

Northampton

Huntingdon

Thetford

Eye

Dunwich

Worcester

Sherborne

Bury St Edmunds

Hereford

Buckingham

Bedford

Cambridge

Ipswich

Sudbury

Ipswich

Colchester

Gloucester

Pembroke

Swansea

Cirencester

Malmesbury

Oxford

Cricklade

Wallingford

London

Cardiff

Castle Combe

Bristol

Bath

Marlborough

Southwark

Trowbridge

Watchet

Salisbury

Canterbury

Sandwich

Wivelescombe

Taunton

Shaftesbury

Winchester

Bramber

Dover

Ilchester

Wilton

Steyning

Lewes

Rye

Southampton

Chichester

Hastings

Dorchester

Exeter

Wareham

Pevensey

Launceston

5 Production in a time of conflict

Does money fail? – come to my mint – coin paper.

Percy Bysshe Shelley

Production of currency during war can be a challenging undertaking. Supplies of bullion can either no longer be available or become so limited that other materials have to be used. The opposite, however, has also been experienced, with windfalls of bullion, captured or given in ransoms, adding to existing stocks. State mints, as previously mentioned (Chapter 3, pp. 54-7), can struggle to keep up with increases in demand for currency or new mints have to be set up, sometimes following the course of an itinerant monarch or an advancing army. Where previously there was routine and stability there now comes improvisation, the long-held sanctities of processes and standards giving way to the art of the possible.

Left. Map showing the mints operating during the reign of Stephen under his authority, as well as that of Empress Matilda and the regional barons.

Multiple mints

Usually governments maintain a tight grip on their monopoly to furnish a population with ready cash and more often than not extract handsome fees through the manufacturing process. Neither the authority to mint nor the profits arising are ever willingly relinquished but war changes the rules of the game. A weakening of state control can allow the usurper or regional power to assume responsibility for making money. England was disfigured by conflict during the civil war of Stephen's reign and central control over the coinage broke down. The country became divided between those areas loyal to Stephen and those supporting his opponents who had pledged allegiance to his cousin Empress Matilda, mostly located in the west of England and Wales. In twelfth-century England there was a well-established network of regional mints overseen from the centre but during this time of unrest coins were issued in the name of Matilda as well as under the authority of several of her supporters. The fragmentation in monetary control was reflected in the quality of coins emanating from regional mints, which were often poorly struck or underweight, and production of pieces from defaced dies of Stephen's official coinage spoke out as an act of defiance. A national coinage system was restored after the settlement of the civil war from 1153 but the episode demonstrates how keenly the right to mint is picked up when the opportunity arises.

During the wars of the Catholic League in France towards the end of the sixteenth century opposing sides issued coins at temporary mints under their control. Most of the large cities held out for the League which meant the royalists had to open their own mints at locations nearby, resulting in coins being produced at Compiègne close to Paris, at Dieppe instead of Rouen and Sémur en Auxois several miles north west of Dijon. Supporters of the Catholic League opened temporary mints too but for all this moving about the resulting coinage remained reasonably consistent.

Another civil war, this time in the 1640s, shares points of similarity with the domestic strife experienced by Stephen in the twelfth century but there is a sense under Charles I of matters being a little more orderly than in the 1140s. After he left London on 10th January 1642, access to the Mint in the Tower was denied to Charles so forces loyal to him established mints in support of his military campaigns against the parliamentarians. There was already a mint operating under the authority of the king in Aberystwyth prior to the beginning of the war and, in September 1642, its equipment was transferred to Shrewsbury where a mint was established in connection with the recruitment of soldiers for the king's army. Royalist mints were subsequently set up in Oxford, Bristol, Truro, Exeter, York and Chester, and it is thought in other locations too, although the attribution of coins to specific towns has not always been conclusively established. Local populations, as in besieged towns, contributed silver plate which was duly melted down and, apart from the mint at York where machines were used, the metal was turned into coins using the same hand-striking methods of production as were employed at the Tower. There was variety in the standard to which the coins were made and many were poorly produced, but as a series their quality holds up reasonably well given the temporary nature of how the mints operated. Although the amount of coins issued by this network was small compared to the number already in circulation, it was nonetheless a useful supplement.

Availability of ready cash in centres close to military activity, or where soldiers were being recruited, dictated the locations but sometimes other motivations were at work. The output at Oxford included large and elaborately designed triple unites in gold, suggesting Charles was using access to a mint to promote the ongoing prestige of his kingship. That there was a public-relations purpose in mind is given added weight through images of the coin appearing in a royalist pamphlet titled *A Warning Piece* printed in Oxford in February 1643.

Above. Spectacular triple unite of Charles I produced at his mint in Oxford.

Multiple mints, whether in times of peace or war, gave way gradually during the early modern period to a single centralised operation which by the twentieth century had become a complex factory supported by sophisticated distribution networks. During the nineteenth century the Royal Mint bucked the trend by establishing branch mints, albeit on an international scale, in Australia and in the early twentieth century in Canada and South Africa. Their locations were determined not by war but by proximity to gold mines, the exception being the branch established for one year only in Bombay which struck sovereigns in 1918 to supply the British army.

Sources of metal

The supply of raw materials with which to make coins in temporary locations could present a problem. Charles I's triple unite noted above was said to have been the product of melted down gold chains of office and jewellery. But, as this instance itself demonstrates, war can create the opportunity to access bullion not usually available.

One such source was to be found in the form of ransoms. Particularly in the medieval period, a country would pay to secure the release of a captured monarch in its own currency, only to find the same being melted down to make the coins of the opposing territory. In 1194 Richard I (1189-99) paid a substantial weight of silver coins to Duke Leopold V of Austria (1177-94) to buy his freedom. The Austrian leader went on to strike coins from the bullion which, it is claimed, resulted in the founding of the Austrian Mint. Edward III (1327-77) was successful in extracting large ransoms from, amongst others, John II of France (1350-64) and David II of Scotland (1329-71), and while by no means all, or even the greater part, was melted down to make English coins, the Mint in the Tower benefitted from this additional supply. If not strictly ransom payments, the practice of Anglo-Saxon rulers paying Vikings to leave them in peace, known as Danegeld, can certainly be placed in the category of military extortion. One of the outcomes is that English coins of the period are sometimes to be found in greater numbers in Scandinavia than in England.

The more deliberate capture of gold and silver from an enemy has acted as a supplementary source of metal for coinage, one of the better documented occasions being the seizure in 1702 of bullion by British forces at Vigo Bay in north west Spain. What was recovered from the Spanish ships was brought back to London and, to draw attention to the successful action, silver and gold coins were produced with the word 'Vigo' placed beneath the bust of Queen Anne (1702-14). The Spanish had actually removed most of the bullion from their own treasure ships prior to the arrival of the British fleet, so the glorious action was not in reality all that noteworthy, but the authorities in London were not about to let the truth stand in the way of a good story.

Beneficiaries of one age transform, in time, into the victims of another. The British ocean liner SS *Laurentic* was carrying 43 tonnes of gold from Liverpool to Halifax, Nova Scotia, in 1917 when it was sunk by a German submarine off the coast of Ireland. During the Second World War Germany, on more than one occasion, captured or destroyed bullion destined for British shores. On its journey back from India in February 1941 the SS *Gairsoppa* was torpedoed by a German U-boat off the Irish coast. Part of its cargo was £600,000 of silver destined for the Royal Mint. At the time the loss had to be made up by other means but a successful salvage operation in 2011 returned back to dry land 2792 ingots, almost all the insured silver on board. In a poignant footnote to the story, some of it finally found its way to the Mint to be turned into silver commemorative coins bearing the name of the ship on the edge. Then, as part of an episode of the BBC television programme *Coast*, specimens of the coins were presented to the granddaughter of Richard Ayres, the only man to survive the *Gairsoppa*'s sinking, and the now elderly sister and brother, Betty and Denis Driver, who rescued him off the Lizard Peninsula in Cornwall.

The export side of matters also suffered. Efforts to transport silver coins from Britain to Rhodesia in May 1942 were undone when the merchant ship the SS *Benvrackie* was torpedoed off the west coast of Africa. Shipments of one cent coins for Hong Kong were intercepted by the Japanese as part of a policy of imposing use of its own currency in the territory during the Second World War. Local Hong Kong coins were sent to Japan to be melted down, nickel being especially favoured by armaments factories. Knowledge of this led to an order for over four million nickel five-cent pieces being cancelled after almost half of them had been made by two mints in Birmingham. The coins were melted down before they ever left British shores. After the war the resulting shortage of metallic currency in Hong Kong had to be addressed through the issue of large amounts of paper money.

Left. Vigo five-guinea piece of Queen Anne, 1703.

Below Left. Painting of the raid by British ships at Vigo Bay in 1702. (© Rijksmuseum, Amsterdam.)

Below. Ingot of silver recovered from the *Gairsoppa* in the salvage operation by Odyssey Marine Exploration.

Debasement and alternative materials

How much precious metal a currency might contain at any one point can be a barometer, if not entirely reliable, of whether a country is at war. During the Hundred Years War, fought between England and France between 1337 and 1453, trade was massively disrupted and in an attempt to relieve indebtedness successive French kings resorted to debasing the silver coinage. Philip VI (1328-50) adulterated the fine silver gros tournois and in the 1350s John II resorted to secret debasements.

In the early stages of the Thirty Years War in central Europe, there was a sudden outbreak of competitive debasement by the imperial and princely territorial mints. Vast numbers of very debased coins were produced in this so-called kipper-und-wipper time, 1620-4. There were profits to be made for a while but as the quantity of precious metal in the coins declined their ready circulation was hindered by a loss of confidence, money-changers hoarding the better pieces while others were heavily clipped.

Above. Gros à la queue of John II, who progressively debased the French coinage during the Hundred Years War. (Courtesy of John Porteous.)

Below. Debased silver coin produced in Bohemia during the early years of the Thirty Years War, enlarged. (Courtesy of John Porteous.)

It was a brief and chaotic episode which ended as suddenly as it had begun. Matters returned to the pre-war arrangements but the period has continued to puzzle historians.

Some centuries later Germany experienced debasement of a different nature stimulated by the armaments industry demanding metals of all kinds during the First World War. The requirement for copper and nickel in the manufacture of guns and shells led the country to turn to iron for its lower denomination five and ten pfennig pieces. Scarcity of metals resulted, almost inevitably, in their prices increasing, which led to one krone notes being issued in Denmark and paper currency of smaller denominations than would normally be expected were printed in the Netherlands for the same reason. Zinc came to be used in the Second World War to make one, five and ten reichspfennig coins which circulated throughout Germany and in occupied territories. It was also employed as a wartime expedient in several other countries, including France, Belgium and the Netherlands. In making cupro-nickel coins for other countries in the 1940s the Royal Mint had to resort to an alloy containing less nickel because of disruption to supplies and British bronze coins of the period were made with slightly less tin arising from shortages.

If being denied access to the usual sources of metal was not bad enough, Iceland during the Second World War was denied access to its usual mint. Having previously been part of Denmark, Iceland had turned to the mint in Copenhagen for its coinage needs but the fall of Denmark to Germany required the authorities in Reykjavik to look elsewhere. They turned to the Mint in London. Orders for the full range of denominations followed, with the first day of production, appropriately, taking place as a chill wind blew through the Mint – the consequence of the roof and windows having been damaged by enemy action the night before.

Above. German ten-pfennig piece made from iron during the First World War.

Below. French twenty centimes of 1942, just one of many zinc coins issued by a number of European countries during the Second World War.

Supporting the war effort

An often higher demand for coinage at a time when raw materials were in short supply was a perfect storm of inconvenience for mint authorities, added to which employees were called upon to contribute to the war effort by joining the armed forces. Some did not return and, as with many organisations, the Mint in London erected a memorial bearing the names of those who died, both on the front line and as a result of enemy bombing of the site. In addition, between 1914 and 1917 the skills of the workforce were directed to the manufacture of precision equipment, such as dials, automatic balances and gauges, a pattern of commitments repeated during war twenty-five years later. The munitions work of the mint in Pretoria grew so large that manufacture of coinage became a fraction of its overall operations and this change of focus was one of the reasons it ceased to be a branch of the Royal Mint from 1941.

Right. Bombs scarred the front of the Mint building at Tower Hill during the Second World War.

Ensuring the continuous supply of money was regarded as a strategic national concern and because mints and central banks are often to be found in capital cities they were regarded as vulnerable to enemy attack. The risk was mitigated in France during the First World War when the state mint was re-located to Castelsarrasin in the Department of Tarn-et-Garonne in the south of the country. Silver one and two franc coins were struck there and carry the letter C as a mintmark to identify where they were made.

In 1938 the Bank of England started making preparations for wartime evacuation by transferring some of the work of the printing department to Overton in Hampshire to be closer to Portals, the Bank's sole supplier of security paper. Two large buildings, which became known as 'shadow factories', were erected adjoining Portals and later other functions of the Bank made their way to the countryside to safeguard continuity of operations.

Left. A printing press in operation at the Bank of England's war-time base in Overton, Hampshire. (Courtesy of the Bank of England Archive, ref. 15A13/15/131.)

Below. Halfpennies for Ireland, ten fils for Iraq and half-sol pieces for Peru were made at Pinewood Studios during the Second World War.

Lloyd's of London moved into the mansion house on the site of Pinewood Studios in Buckinghamshire a few days before hostilities started in September 1939 and the vast unused sound stages provided ideal storage facilities for the government for large amounts of sugar and flour. The Royal Mint soon followed. Its location adjacent to the London Docks meant it was at risk and so, in great secrecy, production of nickel-brass and bronze coins was moved out to Pinewood. The new Mint began operations in June 1941 and, being equipped with furnaces, rolling mills, blanking presses and eight Heaton coining presses, it was entirely self-sufficient. In addition to lower denomination base metal British coins, the temporary facility maintained the international profile of the Mint's commitments by producing coins for Ireland, Iraq and Peru.

In recent years the studio had been struggling and the joke went around that now it was no longer making any films it was finally making money. It was not true, though, to claim no films were being made at Pinewood. Wartime documentaries, like Frank Capra's *Tunisian Victory* (1944), were produced there and employees of the Mint, as well as Lloyd's, found themselves sharing the site with an active film-making community, including a young Richard Attenborough, who was stationed at Pinewood between 1943 and 1946. He starred with Edward G. Robinson in the 1945 RAF film *Journey Together* which was produced at the studios.

Above and right. Maria Theresa thaler produced by the Royal Mint, (right) enlarged.

For additional protection, a set of master tools for the British coinage was lodged with the Bank of England and the precaution of relocating at least part of its production proved a wise move in view of the direct hits sustained by the Mint, the damage to the grand façade still visible today from the patched-up sections of Portland Stone.

As well as mints relocating, currencies have found themselves being made in new places during wars. Maria Theresa thalers, as noted earlier (Chapter 4, p. 64), were an important part of the economy of Ethiopia, and many other countries, particularly in the Middle East, actively used the coin as part of their everyday currency arrangements. Mussolini's efforts to impose Italian rule on Ethiopia included targeting the silver coin and to that end he put pressure on the Austrian government to give up the dies used to make it. Millions, as a result, were minted in Rome between 1935 and 1937, leading the Royal Mint to strike them for several years from 1936, justified on the grounds of providing support for British traders who had been cut off from their usual supplies emanating from Vienna. Other countries followed suit in making their own version of the thaler and so the quintessentially peripatetic coin came to be manufactured in a multinational network of mints.

Production being carried out in makeshift facilities or having to resort to unusual alloys has led to changes in the way currencies look. Alterations in design have also been manifest during or after a war but conflict as an abiding cultural theme has meant images of combat have become embedded as archetypes irrespective of the belligerent habits of a country. Images of war, therefore, have come to permeate the familiar objects used as money, retained by habit as well as adopted through conquest.

6 Images of war on currency

*Money, I think, is uncontrollable.
Even those of us who have it,
we can't control it.*

Martin Amis

An armour-clad soldier wielding a sword has been one of the more obvious ways in which to capture the idea of conflict through the medium of currency design. The ancient world provides many examples and placing the combatant on a horse, in a chariot or on a ship has offered other visual outlets for the same theme. Care should be exercised, however, in always assuming a man holding a sword was referencing victory in a particular battle or of carrying any meaning beyond symbolising the princely attributes of strength and courage. Moreover, the impact of war on the design of money, both paper and metal, goes beyond the depiction of an angry looking warrior and is discernible in less conspicuously confrontational ways. The adoption of the portrait of a victorious leader, the use of an inscription or enlisting the support of national emblems can encapsulate a message of regime change just as powerfully.

Left. Gold noble of Edward III, showing the figure of the king conspicuously carrying a large sword and shield, enlarged.

Above. Silver baudekin, two-thirds of a gros, issued in the name of the Countess of Hainault. (Courtesy of John Porteous.)

Right. Original plaster model by Gilbert Ledward RA for the Coronation crown of 1953.

Monarchs and the imagery of war

The image of a monarch on money is accepted and expected. Those of Elizabeth II on notes and coins are probably the most reproduced likenesses in the history of mankind and today, when viewed alongside those of earlier times, they stand reasonably unadorned. She is not encased in armour, she does not carry a sword or shield and she has not been placed on the deck of a battleship or the turret of a tank. An exception is the Coronation crown of 1953 on which the Queen is shown riding a horse dressed in the uniform of the Colonel-in-Chief of the Grenadier Guards, a familiar sight from her presence at the ceremony of Trooping the Colour. But there was in this choice, as in the nature of the coin itself, a strong dose of ritual.

The use of horses and riders as part of coinage design has a long tradition. A horseman carrying a sword is seen on silver coins issued under the authority of the Countess of Hainault (1244-80) in the Low Countries. The design on the obverse is of a mounted knight dressed in armour, probably inspired by the appearance of such devices on seals of the nobility. A more usual form of ornamentation for a monarch would have been a sceptre but this was far from always the case. During his reign as Prince of Aquitaine between 1362 and 1372, Edward the Black Prince issued silver demi-gros which show him holding a drawn sword, while the spectacular gold four doblas of Henry IV of Castile and Leon (1454-74) place the king on an elaborate throne similarly armed.

For England's first reliable gold coinage, the noble, issued under Edward III from the 1340s, the dual messages of strength in trade and arms was being promoted. As with the florin of Florence and the genovino of Genoa, the introduction of new coins was directed at helping the mercantile class but the image on the English noble was of a ship in which the king is brandishing a sword and holding a shield. Its relatively high value meant that it will have played a role in domestic and overseas trade but its design could be interpreted as a reference to the English naval victory over France at the battle of Sluys in 1340, four years before the coin was first issued. If true, it would

certainly have appealed to a sense of English nationalism. In the hands of a monarch, though, a sword carries more than a purely military meaning; as well as being a symbol of defending the realm it has significance as the sword of justice and with both in mind it plays a ceremonial role at coronations.

The noble formed part of a tentative trend towards more elaborately drawn pictorial designs, particularly on gold coins, apparent from the mid-fourteenth century. Under the Tudors it advanced further with royal iconography being re-imagined during the first half of the sixteenth century through realistic portraiture. The reign of Edward VI provides spectacular examples, capturing the face of a young, sometimes vulnerable looking, king. He was a frail child and perhaps to compensate he is shown on gold sovereigns dressed in an elaborately decorated suit of armour holding a sword. Edward is also encountered on silver crowns and half-crowns on a caparisoned horse, sword again in hand, the first English king to be represented in this way. James I, too, was fond of being

portrayed on horseback, immediately conveying a sense of vigour and not a little theatre. James chose to accompany his coins with forthright inscriptions, such as *Exurgat deus et dissipentur inimici*, let the Lord arise and let his enemies be scattered, an established phrase borrowed from the medieval Scottish coinage. If use of this type of imagery was being influenced by familiar forms, it nonetheless carried a message of power and authority but the depiction of James's son, Charles I, in the same equestrian pose was infused much more explicitly with meaning following the outbreak of the English Civil War.

The portraits by Thomas Rawlins of Charles shown mounted are amongst the most memorable of English coinage designs. Chief amongst them is the Oxford crown of 1644 but perhaps more dramatic is the silver twenty shillings of 1642 on which the king, somewhat formal in posture, is shown trampling over a collection of arms and armour. Almost as visually arresting is the use made of inscriptions on his coinage in bold horizontal lines, proclaiming his purpose: devotion to the Protestant religion, the

Opposite. Gold sovereign of Edward VI.

Opposite below. Silver crown of James I bearing an authoritative equestrian portrait on one side and a traditional, if somewhat belligerent, religious message on the other.

Below. The unwieldy silver twenty-shilling piece of Charles I showing the king riding over broken up armour.

Above. Half-crown struck at the Bristol mint in 1644 bearing a prominent inscription declaring Charles I's political aims.

Below. Gold unite issued under the authority of the Commonwealth.

Right. Handsomely proportioned half-crown of Cromwell's last unissued coinage, enlarged.

laws of the land and the liberty of Parliament. At the time it might have seemed like a manifesto, and it was, but for those serving with Charles, like his nephew Prince Rupert who fought on the continent in the Thirty Years War, the approach would have been familiar from European coinages of the time which were heavily inscriptional in their style.

In the setting of a country tearing itself apart in the 1640s there were signs of deep conservatism alongside acts of extremism and radical thought. Cromwell's forces, despite their control of the national Mint in the Tower, continued to issue coins bearing the portrait of the king they were seeking to defeat, their sense of reserve driven by a wish to project legitimacy and a reluctance to usurp royal authority. Even after the execution of Charles in January 1649 the coinage of the Commonwealth might be regarded as traditional in following the existing weight and denominational structure but in design there was a radical departure. Known at the time as 'harp and cross money' on account of its appearance, it was spare and shorn of any trace of ornate decoration, the Puritan influence strongly defining its appearance. The inscriptions were now in English rather than Latin, portraiture was abandoned and in its place the most heraldic of coinages was conceived bearing shields on both sides, strongly focusing on the cross of St George. But towards the end of Cromwell's time as Lord Protector there were proposals for a complete reversion to the royalist style. Designs were prepared on which Cromwell's portrait dominates the obverse, wreathed and encircled by Latin titles, looking every bit the monarch or even Roman emperor. It was an unexpected image in more ways than one, the only precedent for wreathed portraits on English coins being those of James I on gold laurels from earlier in the century. The care with which they were designed suggests a clear intent to issue but there is no evidence they were ever released.

Not every leader comes to power by force of arms, and so not every change of likeness on coins and notes has a military cause but, for those who do, currency has offered a ready means of expression for promoting their new status. Napoleon made ample use of his likeness as his armies assimilated European states during the first decade of the nineteenth century. New coins were issued in Italian territories in Napoleon's name and carried a well-proportioned classically inspired bust of the ambitious emperor. In these instances it was not the weapons of war that defined the military significance of the coins but the sudden appearance of a different face staring back at the people of the conquered lands.

Depiction of conflict

Coinage design at its best has tended towards the emblematic. Prior to the advent of modern collector coins, it would have been a vain search amongst national coinages for the elaboration of detailed battle scenes, a genre of numismatic art more frequently encountered on the larger canvases of official and commemorative medals which form no meaningful part of this study. But when pictorial scenes do come into play they have often focused on conflict.

Religion, probably more than war, finds a place in the conventions of coinage design through crosses and inscriptional pledges. But the two become joined in the European tradition of representing patron saints on coins, as with the image of St Michael killing a serpent on English gold angels from the mid-fifteenth century. The addition of renaissance-style armour in place of feathers from the reign of Henry VII makes St Michael seem even more intent on his purpose. England's patron saint, George, arrives on the English coinage in 1526 under Henry VIII on the short-lived George noble. It was a splendid creation, a charging heavily armoured knight, the plain cross of St George emblazoned on his chest, thrusting a lance into the open mouth of a prostrate dragon. St Michael and St George are engaged in the eternal struggle, the war of good against evil. Both these encounters position conflict in the spiritual

Above. Fifteen soldi issued by Napoleon following his conquest of Italy.

Left. The George noble of Henry VIII carries a sophisticated treatment of St George killing the dragon, enlarged.

Below. The third type of Treasury one pound note issued during the First World War from 1917.

realm but, particularly with St George, the reference is also to chivalry and the Order of the Garter. Such imagery would have carried a clear meaning in the context of England as a feudal state probably more so than as an allusion to Henry VIII's war against France.

St George is by no means exclusively to be found in an English setting. He is seen on Crusader coins of Roger, Prince of Antioch, in the twelfth century, but much more regularly he is met with charging across German thalers from the sixteenth century. His revival on the British sovereign from 1817 in the fading years of George III's reign led eventually to St George becoming synonymous with this particular gold coin. The imagery associated with the chivalric Order of St George is to be found on silver crowns, half-crowns and shillings at different points throughout the nineteenth century, represented by the garter belt accompanied by the inscription *Honi soit qui mal y pense*, evil to him who thinks evil of it.

Banknotes have not unreasonably made use of the same stock of national emblems. When the Bradbury Treasury notes were issued from 1914 they carried a small image of St George placed in the

garter belt. Versions of the notes from later in the war carried much larger and elaborate treatments of the classic myth, perhaps chosen as a deliberate visual point of reference with the gold coinage to encourage their acceptance. In the 1920s, St George, as he appears on the sovereign, was used on the reverse of coloured banknotes, anchoring clearly the link with gold as backing for paper money. As the Bank of England came to explore ever more colourful approaches, St George slaying his dragon was placed in the centre of twenty-pound notes issued between 1970 and 1993.

Female symbols of a country are by no means always concerned with the military side of state affairs. The French La Semeuse is seeking to generate new life as the sower, while Lady Liberty suggests for the United States the rule of law is of the utmost importance. For Britain, though, for more than 300 years, the figure of Britannia has been prominently employed to represent the nation. In her most familiar form she wears a Corinthian helmet, carries a spear and sits with a shield on one side and, sometimes, a lion on the other. She is the defence of Britain personified and has been called upon to take part in military

Above. Artwork by Harry Eccleston for the Bank of England Series D twenty-pound note first issued in 1970. (© Governor and Company of the Bank of England.)

Below. Back of the Bank of England's first colour one pound note issued from November 1928.

Above. Copper halfpenny of Charles II, 1672, depicting Britannia on the reverse.

campaigns through the medium of coinage and medal design. The first English coins carrying an image of Britannia are copper halfpennies and farthings issued under Charles II in 1672. A pattern piece, struck a little while earlier, carried the somewhat provocative inscription *Quattuor Maria Vindico*, I claim the four seas, to which the Dutch, with whom England was then fighting, might well have taken exception. She is a benign looking figure but has the military props of spear and shield, derived directly from the coins of Hadrian, albeit alongside a prominently positioned sprig of olive. The appearance of a trident in her hand and a ship on the horizon on Matthew Boulton's copper coinage of 1797 has been interpreted as a more defiant portrayal, coinciding with the war between Britain and France. Just over a hundred years later, during the reign of Edward VII (1901-10), Britannia was sculpted by George W. De Saulles for the florin, standing defiantly on the prow of what looks like a Nordic longboat. The coin was issued in the wake of a colonial war in South Africa, the campaign medals for which De Saulles also designed, where he gave Britannia the role of beckoning British soldiers on to fight. In the building tension of the 1930s, though, the placement of a modern warship beside Britannia on proposed designs for pennies of Edward VIII (1936) was judged a step too far. It was removed before the abdication and therefore found no place on the coinage of George VI (1936-52) issued the following year.

The association of Britannia with English banknotes dates back almost as long as her appearance on English coins. Adopted by the Bank of England as a symbol from its foundation in 1694, Britannia is shown sitting beside a large pile of coins and was to have a continuing presence on the nation's notes from that time on. She was for many years the only pictorial element on notes, and as such occupied an important role in the prevention of counterfeiting. On the modern series of polymer banknotes she is still present, figuratively representing continuity, connecting this technically advanced paper currency with the Bank's origins over 300 years ago.

Initially Britannia had been excluded from the decimal coins revealed in 1968. The resulting outcry led to a hasty reassessment of the situation and a place being found for her on the fifty pence piece. There is a chance that Britannia's removal from the design of circulating coins in 2008 may, in generations to come, be judged to have some wider geopolitical significance but by 2015 she was back on two-pound coins designed by sculptor Antony Dufort. The re-introduction came at a time when war as a theme was being explored extensively on United Kingdom commemorative coins but this trend had more to do with a wish to mark anniversaries of past wars than as a response to contemporary events.

Above. Detail from the back of the Bank of England ten-shilling note issued in 1961.

Below. Electrotype of a proposed design for the penny of Edward VIII, showing a battleship to the right of Britannia.

Above. A United Kingdom florin and an Irish ten pence piece stamped with the initials of Northern Ireland paramilitary groups.

Right. Original model by sculptor Clive Duncan for the Battle of Trafalgar commemorative crown piece of 2005.

Modern acts of commemoration

Placing the emblems of a nation on currency has meant coins and notes have come to stand for a territory which in times of conflict has led to their becoming targets. Countermarking has in many instances been intended as an endorsement, often of coins from another country, but the motivation behind certain marks can in no way be seen as anything other than provocative. During the troubles in Northern Ireland both sides took to stamping the initials of paramilitary organisations into coins. For supporters of the Irish Republican Army (IRA), in its opposition to the British state, the solution was to stamp those same initials over the portrait of Elizabeth II. In the hands of the Unionists, it was the Irish coinage that was targeted and, as well as UVF, the Ulster Volunteer Force, the dates of key moments in Northern Irish history were used, such as 1690 – the date of Protestant William III's victory over Catholic James II at the Battle of the Boyne. Similar activities re-emerged in the 1990s with the appearance of RIRA, standing for the Real Irish Republican Army, impressed into British coins in response to the Good Friday Agreement.

The trend, however, in recent decades has more typically been towards commemorating war, both on circulating and collector coins, a shift which started in earnest in 1994 with the issue of a fifty pence piece to mark the fiftieth anniversary of the D-Day Landings. The design by sculptor John Mills was an elegant framing of the landing craft and aerial support planes, and its pictorial treatment was to signal something of a change of direction in the design of United Kingdom coins (Chapter 4, p. 71). There followed in its wake commemorative issues, that had their circulating counterparts, on themes relating to other Second World War anniversaries and through the last twenty-five years Britain's military history has been traversed from the sinking of the *Mary Rose*, through the Battles of Trafalgar and Waterloo, key personalities such as Nelson and Churchill, on to an extensive series from 2014 exploring the centenary of the First World War.

Having more than thirty silver coins in the series has permitted the narrative, human stories and legacy of that conflict to be told, at times in an unflinching manner.

The 100th anniversary of the Armistice in the autumn of 2018 is being marked by the release of other special coins, one of which, a two-pound piece by the lettering artist Stephen Raw, has been produced in advance of the occasion. His approach was to focus on the poetry of Wilfred Owen, making use of the moving phrase 'The truth untold, the pity of war' set against a textured background inspired by soil surrounding Owen's grave.

Banknotes, too, in recent decades have explored British history with scientists and writers, composers and humanitarians portrayed in turn on the changing series periodically issued by the Bank of England. With respect to military history, the Duke of Wellington appeared on the back of five-pound notes issued between 1971 and 1991, and Winston Churchill was chosen for the new polymer five-pound note released in September 2016, almost certainly because of his wartime leadership as much as his service to the nation more generally.

What these acts of commemoration reveal is the continuing influence of war. Its impact can be seen most vividly in the years immediately following and currencies can find themselves swept up in the necessary readjustments to peace. But some effects can be of much longer duration, where emergency measures become embedded in a new status quo or when peace offers a chance to make a fresh start with the prospect of more settled conditions.

Below. Detail from a Bank of England series D five-pound note on which Wellington featured prominently. (© Governor and Company of the Bank of England.)

Right. Part of an extensive collection of United Kingdom silver coins issued to commemorate the centenary of the First World War, enlarged.

7 Aftermath

Above. Most pennies issued under William I depict him holding a sceptre but in one type, issued towards the end of his reign, he is shown holding a sword. (Courtesy of Spink.)

Right. Harold II (1066) swearing an oath of fealty to William of Normandy on holy relics, 1064. William used this oath to support his claim to the English throne. Bayeux Tapestry, 1067. (© World History Archive/Alamy stock photograph.)

After the guns have fallen silent returning soldiers need to be re-employed, control over inflation often has to be re-established and the reputation of a currency sometimes re-built. If the war in question involved changes in design or in the materials used to make coins and banknotes then questions arise over whether they should be jettisoned or absorbed into a new settlement.

The impact of regime change

The most prominent conquest in English history was that effected by William, Duke of Normandy, in 1066 but its impact on the coinage was not at all memorable. A profound sense of continuity pervades his approach to affairs concerning the design and manufacture of English money. Reform of the coinage impacting upon how it looked, how much it weighed or what it was made of was not evident. There was, as noted earlier (Chapter 4, p. 61), a marked increase in hoarding but effigies of him wielding a sword,

looking like a conqueror, are absent from all but one of the types of coins issued under his name. It also did not occur to him to reduce the standard of English coins to the rather poor condition of those circulating in Normandy; rather, he did what most successful conquerors do and absorbed what he found to his own purpose.

For Charles II, though, matters were somewhat more pointed. After he returned to London he had Cromwell's body dug up and his head placed on a spike in Westminster. His treatment of the Commonwealth coinage was no less brutal. On 7th September 1661 he ordered it to be demonetised by November of that year and thereafter only exchangeable at the Mint for the same value in regal money. Somewhat ironically, though, the royal image he chose for his coinage looked far more like that of Cromwell on his final unissued series than of Charles I.

Revolutionaries responsible for dismantling regimes have a tendency to bear an uncanny resemblance, after a period of time, to those they have overthrown and the continuing use of an opponent's money can make a great deal of sense from

a practical point of view. For the American colonies fighting for independence from Britain between 1775 and 1783, however, the idea of taking a consciously different approach was important. Britain had outlawed the printing of paper currency by the colonies and in the years leading up to the struggle for independence this was one of the many acts of interference which stoked resentment. Once war had started the imperial restraints were ignored and the issue of a new form of paper currency, which became known as Continental Currency, was one of the first acts authorised by Congress. The opportunity was not lost to inspire the fight by creating designs carrying inspirational images of a pastoral idyll. Not only did it provide a means through which the colonies could fund the war but it also gave them the beginnings of freedom from British monetary control over their affairs, further evidence of which was provided by the return of guineas to Britain in large numbers after the war. For the newly independent United States the creation of its own money became a key part of the country's identity which might account for why authority to issue money was placed in Article 1 of the American Constitution.

Below. Continental Currency twenty dollar bill, printed during the American War of Independence. (Courtesy of the Colonial Williamsburg Foundation, gift of the Lasser family.)

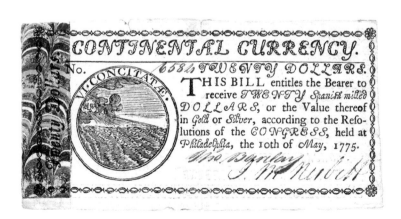

As Britain looked for a new empire, expanding the area of its influence during the nineteenth century, its forces came armed with monetary traditions which were imposed in Africa and the Caribbean, alongside the use of existing forms of currency. It was at times a tricky balance because of the long-held familiarity, for example in the West Indies, with using Spanish silver dollars and Portuguese gold doubloons. From 1825 the imperial influence was strongly felt practically and symbolically throughout the empire when concerted attempts were made to impose use of silver in British territories and also when the gold sovereign, particularly in the second half of the century, started to circulate freely. As the use of the Spanish dollar declined, the area of the world falling under the influence of sterling expanded substantially and, as a consequence, an increasing proportion of the Royal Mint's work came to be devoted to making quantities of British currency actively used overseas, as well as colonial coinages.

In the first two decades of the twentieth century dramatic changes of regimes and the beginnings of empires came thick and fast but sometimes the release of coins and notes to represent the new states lagged behind the dramatic revolutions or struggles for independence. During the period of War Communism immediately following the socialist revolution in Russia of 1917 there was an attempt to abolish money altogether propounded by the All-Russian Central Executive Committee. It was still being advanced as a policy in 1920 but the necessity of a banking system and a currency prevailed. The Soviet Union was not formally established until 1922 and when coins of a distinctively Soviet style arrived from 1924 the imagery of some, such as the silver half-rouble, captured the identity and ideology of the system of government through robustly idealised depictions of ordinary workers labouring on behalf of the state. The designs were, moreover, markedly different from those of Nicholas II (1894-1917) which sat firmly in the European tradition of portraiture and heraldry. During their revolutionary struggles Bolshevik authorities accused Britain of

Above. Portuguese gold doubloon of 1707.

Below and left. Silver half-rouble of 1924 (below), one of the first coins issued by the Soviet Union, and (left) a nickel-faced electrotype for the reverse.

counterfeiting Russian imperial banknotes, but an indication of the primacy currency demand can have over politics is provided a few years later when the Soviet government placed an order for the manufacture of half-roubles with the Royal Mint in London.

There are elements of similarity with the Irish Free State. Having secured independence from Britain in 1921, following a bitterly fought conflict, Eire finally issued its exemplary series of coins in 1928, all made by the enemy from whom it had just secured freedom. As with the first Soviet coins, the opportunity to make a statement of identity on such readily used objects was not lost and the designs, based on the country's strong farming traditions, have come to be regarded as classics of modern numismatic art.

These episodes reveal the complexities within which currency operates, needing on the one hand stability of standards and systems, while on the other seeking to be distinctive and represent identity in unambiguous ways. In the aftermath of a war such issues can become blurred and so it was that sterling continued to be accepted in an independent Ireland for over fifty years to the end of the 1970s.

Latvia offers a further insight into the long-lasting impact of imagery generated through a struggle for independence. As a territory it had come under Russian and German influence successively for an extended period but in 1918 it secured independence from Russia. The design of the resulting currency included a large five-lati silver coin issued from 1929 which bore the image of a traditional Latvian maiden. Struck, as many other new European currencies were at the time, by a commercially minded Royal Mint in London, it came to represent Latvian freedom during the Soviet re-occupation in the 1940s and was treasured by

Below. Original plaster model for the Latvian five-lati silver coin.

many as an object with almost devotional reverence. When officials from the Latvian central bank visited Britain in May 2012 to see what had been retained of the artwork and tooling for their coinage, their emotional reaction on seeing the original low-relief sculpture for the five-lati was not dissimilar to pilgrims paying homage at a reliquary.

Monetary reform

Systems of currency do not always change as a result of war and that can apply even to major international conflicts. France was not compelled to start using pounds, shillings and pence after Waterloo and Germany was not forced to adopt sterling or the dollar after the First or Second World Wars. But there are instances in which the ending of a conflict can lead to the release of pent-up demands for reform that find an outlet in the atmosphere of peace and the hope for a fresh start.

So it was in 1816-17 when Britain decided to overhaul its currency system following the end of its long war with France in 1815. The reforms involved the withdrawal and recoining of silver, the release of a gold sovereign of twenty shillings and placing Britain formally on the gold standard. In the conditions of a post-Waterloo world, the introduction of such an extensive series of changes was much more palatable than they could ever have been while fighting Napoleon and the success of the new settlement thereafter was in no small measure the consequence of Britain's advance as an economic and military power.

A century later there was undoubtedly an expectation that sovereigns would be seen again on the streets of London after the end of the First World War. Following the Treaty of Versailles the minds of British politicians were determined on the idea of a return to a fully operational domestic gold standard, which found formal endorsement through the recommendations of the Cunliffe Committee in 1918. Winston Churchill carried the dubious and reluctant honour as Chancellor in 1925 of establishing sovereigns as a reserve currency but the economic pressures of the late 1920s meant the gold standard had to be abandoned by all major western powers from 1931.

Britain's silver currency did not escape unscathed either. Sustained higher metal prices after the end of hostilities led officials to see no

Below. Half-crown, shilling and sixpence issued as part of the coinage reforms of 1816-17.

Above. Children stand next to a tower of 100,000 marks, equal in value to one United States dollar, 1923. (Courtesy of rarehistoricalphotos.com)

prospect of change any time soon and from 1920 the amount of silver was reduced from the centuries-old 925 sterling standard to an alloy containing only 500 parts per 1000. The fact that the war was over did not make the need to act in this instance any less urgent. A point had been reached in the ascent of the price of silver where the bullion value in the coins was higher than the face value, a situation that could not be tolerated for any meaningful length of time. For Britain's currency the impact of the First World War, both immediate and longer-term, was significant and other countries in Europe experienced challenges in adjusting to the new world order.

During and after the war, inflation stimulated by the over issue of paper currencies was a greater problem in eastern areas of Europe, such as Austria-Hungary, Russia and Poland, than it was in western and southern Europe but the extreme case was Germany. Between 1914 and 1923 prices spiralled out of control. Numerous causes have been advanced but a fair amount of the blame can be laid at the door of financing short-term government borrowing through note issues and also the imposition of swingeing reparations through the terms of the Treaty of Versailles which did nothing to aid the Weimar government's ability to stimulate German economic recovery. The result was one of the most devastating episodes of hyperinflation of any age, captured through images of large quantities of virtually valueless notes being carted about in wheelbarrows or of families burning bundles of them to keep warm. A crippling rate of inflation in Germany was a further consequence of war a generation later, with large increases in public debt aligned to the issue of paper currency. It could be said that in both world wars Germany's financial structure was unable to support the ambitions of its military and political leaders. The fall in the value of its currency, though, turned out to be short lived as the German economy revived and the deutsche mark became one of the world's leading currencies.

Following the end of the Second World War the British coinage was subjected to yet another debasement, this time introduced from 1947 when use of silver in the circulating coinage was abandoned altogether in favour of cupro-nickel. Pressure on this occasion was not so much related to changes in precious metal prices but rather a response to the urgency the United States placed on Britain repaying its war loan to them. The formal end of the lend-lease scheme, which operated between the United States and other Allied countries, imposed a timetable by which loans had to be repaid and one of the ways Britain achieved this was by taking silver out of the nation's pockets – 88 million ounces of it.

Once these major twentieth-century conflicts had passed, the landscape of British currency arrangements had substantially changed from what it had been thirty years earlier. Centuries-old traditions of using precious metals as the basis of everyday exchange had been swept away and on the horizon lay a new order of achieving a balance between notes and coins and eventually credit cards.

The legacy of peace

Struggles against British rule, or the more peaceful relinquishing
of ties, have been one of the richest sources of monetary change in
the last hundred years. Towards the end of the twentieth century a
not dissimilar process took place across eastern Europe. In the years
following the fall of the Berlin Wall in 1989, and the gradual break-up
of the Soviet Union's network of satellite states, there emerged newly
independent countries which set about creating newly independent
currencies. In this instance the war in question was the Cold War
and its end led to a re-awakening of interest in national symbols
and the re-imagining of them on notes and coins issued across
eastern Europe.

But the most prominent theme of post-war European monetary affairs
has been the advent of the Single European Currency. Countries have
used each others coinages readily when it was recognised how their
values and precious-metal content were aligned to trading and domestic
requirements. The ubiquity of the Spanish dollar, the Maria Theresa
thaler and the sovereign is ample testimony to how there can be
understanding and co-operation across borders in currency matters.

Formal monetary unions have also operated. In the Netherlands, during the reign of Philip the Good (1419-67), a form of currency union operated between the states of the region whereby coins of a similar size, bearing a common design on one side, were combined with a state-related design on the other, the same model adopted by the Single Currency. There are similar instances across German states but the Latin Monetary Union, initiated in the 1860s involving France, Belgium, Italy and Switzerland, was the most wide-reaching. For a time it worked, and other countries joined some years later, but it unravelled for all practical purposes from the onset of the First World War.

The unprecedented absence of war between major European powers over the seventy years since 1945 has generated its own monetary legacy. Conflicts are crucibles for change but in the conditions of peace that have obtained in Europe it has been possible for consideration to be given to long-term economic and political plans, one of the most prominent being the establishment of the Single Currency. It was deliberately envisaged as a way of drawing countries together economically and, if it also operated as a means of avoiding war by encouraging closer political ties, then the currency's architects would

Above and below. The Estonian heraldic symbol of three lions was the principal national emblem on the coinage (below, enlarged) from 1991.

have been equally content. Whatever the future holds for the Single Currency, its very existence, scale and longevity could not have been conceived during the centuries of war-making that have defined so much of European history.

Left. Notes of the Single European currency carry the same designs across all countries based on the theme of bridges, whereas the coins are permitted to have a national design on one side.

Death and taxes

Bob Dylan once sang 'money doesn't talk it swears', appropriately enough for the theme of this book, in a song titled *It's alright, Ma (I'm only bleeding)*. One almost imagines money doing both when confronted by war. But in the modern era the more significant episodes of conflict seem to have carried with them much less disruption to the currencies of the world than was the case fifty or a hundred years ago. The decentralising impact of war involving multiple issuers, or the framework of a nation's currency needing to be thoroughly reformed, have not obviously afflicted the world powers through their involvement in either of the Gulf Wars, in the Balkans, the ongoing troubles in Afghanistan, North Africa or Syria. Then again, these have been at times allegedly proxy wars, fought far from their native shores. On the ground, the reality of using money, as was illustrated by the journalist's story of buying beer in the Balkans in the 1990s, can still be one of disruption. Moreover, even though the substance of great-power currencies has remained unscathed in recent times, their value on international money markets has been far from immune. The onset of war many hundreds of miles from Wall Street or the City of London can still make brokers twitchy, can still send oil prices into a flurry, and the age-old ghosts of instability can still stalk the reputation of otherwise bomb-proof currencies.

Quite apart from its appalling toll on life, war has triggered developments in one form or another in most aspects of human activity. The theatre of war has been represented in music and paintings. It has been re-enacted and re-told in novels, poetry, plays and sprawling historical dramas. It has subjected economies and social structures to huge shocks. Money's odyssey has been shaped by war and forms an integral part of its narrative, operating

as a commodity form of exchange at the same time as battles
involved firing cannons and muskets, on into a world in which
the fighter pilot is assisted by every digital aid, just as the
financial and monetary structure keeping his plane in the air
has become no less reliant on computer-driven innovations.
Contactless payments are just about as divorced from the
substance of exchange using valuable bits of metal dug out
of the ground as it is possible to be. Extending technology
across different aspects of a given culture should not be
surprising but the speed and intensity of modern war is
nonetheless at times startling and finds itself reflected in
the velocity of transactions built into the fibre of how the
world operates today.

There remains a profound sense of connectedness between
currency and war. The financial wherewithal to wage war
now is no less a prerequisite of the successful prince or
president as it always has been. For much of the last 500 years
that ability has been funded by debt, cementing an alliance
between money and war, and creating a link with Benjamin
Franklin's timeless observation of 1789 that 'nothing is
certain except death and taxes'.

The most poignant of objects relating to currency in a time
of war are coins that have saved the life of a soldier and carry
the impact of the bullet that would otherwise have been fatal.
It is an unexpected role - loose change becoming chain-mail,
money as armour, coinage as defence. The idea conveyed
through the imagery on coinage is of the monarch as
defender of the faith and protector of the people. Here the
idea is played out of the image of a monarch quite literally
saving the life of a subject. There could be no more powerful
expression of the unlooked for symbolism of currency: icon
of state as defender of the people.

Bibliography

Jennifer Adam, *The First World War and the Bank of England*. Bank of England Museum, 2014.

Scott Anderson, *Lawrence in Arabia: war, deceit, imperial folly and the making of the modern Middle East*. London, 2014.

Stephen B. Baxter, *William III*. London, 1966.

Edward Besly, *Coins and medals of the English Civil War*. Cardiff, 1990.

Roger Bland, *Coin hoards and hoarding in Roman Britain, AD 43-c.498*. London, 2018.

John Brewer, *The sinews of power: war, money and the English state, 1688-1783*. London, 1989.

Morris Bright, *Pinewood Studios: 70 years of fabulous filmmaking*. London, 2007.

Derrick Byatt, *Promises to pay: the first three hundred years of the Bank of England notes*. London, 1994.

C. E. Challis, *The Tudor coinage*. Manchester, 1978.

C. E. Challis (ed.), *A new history of the Royal Mint*. Cambridge, 1992.

Robert Chalmers, *A history of currency in the British colonies*. London, 1893.

Kevin Clancy, *A history of the sovereign: chief coin of the world*. Llantrisant, 2015.

J. H. Clapham, *The Bank of England: a history*. 2 vols. Cambridge, 1944.

B. J. Cook, 'The Royal household and the mint (1279-1399)'. *The Numismatic Chronicle 149* (1989).

J. K. Cooley, *Currency wars: forging money to break economies*. London, 2008.

J. Craig, *The Mint: a history of the London Mint from AD 287 to 1948*. Cambridge, 1953.

Joe Cribb (ed.), *Money: from Cowrie shells to credit cards*. London, 1986.

Joe Cribb, 'Money as metaphor 1-4'. *The Numismatic Chronicle 165-67, 69* (2005-09).

Glyn Davies, *A history of money from ancient times to the present day*. Cardiff, 2002.

P. G. M. Dickson, *The financial revolution in England: a study in the development of public credit 1688-1756*. 2017.

Alfred Draper, *Operation Fish: the race to save Europe's wealth 1939-1945*. London, 1979.

Vincent Duggleby, *English paper money: 300 years of Treasury and Bank of England notes 1694-1994*. 5th edition. London, 1994.

G. P. Dyer, 'The currency crisis of 1797', *British Numismatic Journal 72* (2002).

A. E. Feavearyear, *The pound sterling: a history of English money*. 2nd edition. Oxford, 1963.

Niall Ferguson, *The cash nexus: money and power in the modern world, 1700-2000*. London, 2001.

Adam Fergusson, *When money dies: the nightmare of the Weimar collapse*. London, 1975.

Denis Gray, *Spencer Perceval: the evangelical Prime Minister, 1762-1812*. Manchester, 1963.

Christopher Hibbert, *Wellington: a personal view*. London, 1998.

J. K. Horsefield, *British monetary experiments, 1650-1710*. London, 1960.

Kevin Jackson, (ed.), *The Oxford book of money*. Oxford, 1995.

E. M. Kelly, *Spanish dollars and silver tokens: an account of the issues of the Bank of England 1797-1816*. London, 1976.

Eric Kerridge, *Trade and banking in early modern England*. Manchester, 1988.

John Maynard Keynes, *Economic consequences of peace*. London, 1920.

John Keyworth, Bank of England exhibition booklets.

From gold to paper currency: the suspension of cash payments 1797-1821. 1997.

Amusing, shocking, informing: the Bank of England's Cartoons and Caricatures. 2000

Forgery, the artful crime. 2001.

Business as usual: the Bank of England and its staff during World War II. Unpublished, 2005.

Charles P. Kindleberger, *A financial history of western Europe*. Oxford, 1984.

Charles Larkin, 'The great recoinage of 1696: Charles Davenant and monetary theory', in D. Carey (ed.), *Money and political economy in the Enlightenment*. Oxford, 2014.

Felix Martin, *Money, the unauthorised biography*. London, 2013.

Peter Mathias, *The first industrial nation: an economic history of Britain*. 2nd edition. London, 1983.

N. J. Mayhew, *Sterling: the rise and fall of a currency*. London, 1999.

Patrick O'Brian, *The far side of the world*. London, 1984.

Samuel Pepys, *Diary*. Accessed through www.pepysdiary.com

John Porteous, *Coins in history: a survey of the coinage from the reform of Diocletian to the Latin Monetary Union*. London, 1969.

Stephen Quinn, 'Gold, silver and the Glorious Revolution'. Economic History Review 49, 3 (1996).

Murray N. Rothbard (ed.), *A history of money and banking in the United States: the colonial era to World War II*. Auburn, 2002.

Royal Mint Annual Reports, 1870-1976. London.

Clara Semple, *A silver legend: the story of the Maria Theresa thaler*. Manchester, 2005.

William Shakespeare, *Henry V*.

Hew Strachan, *Financing the First World War*. New York, 2004.

C. H. V. Sutherland, *Art in coinage: the aesthetics of money from Greece to the present day*. London, 1955.

Index

Acknowledgements

The idea of writing a book about the influence war has exercised over money, particularly in the form of coins and banknotes, arose out of a conversation with Emma Howard, Head of Publications at Spink. I am indebted to her for having faith in the proposition from the start and for encouraging me throughout. The Trustees of the Royal Mint Museum, especially Dr Andrew Burnett, have provided the framework within which research on the subject has been carried out, while at the Royal Mint Anne Jessopp and Nicola Howell have continued to support the Museum's publication programme. It would not have been possible to complete this book were it not for the help of my colleague Abigail Kenvyn who has tirelessly tracked down images and offered helpful comments on the text. Sarah Tyley and Susan Sandford have unearthed items from the Royal Mint Museum collection, and Hannah Merry has provided invaluable proof-reading expertise. As with other titles in this series, photographers Andrew Jenkins and Chris Herbert have been creative and professional in enhancing the book's visual appeal.

Edward Besly and Dr Barrie Cook kindly read the manuscript at an early stage and both have directed my attention to useful sources, sparing me from several errors of judgement and fact. I have benefited from conversations with them and with Joe Cribb, Hugh Pagan and Robin Porteous who have been liberal with their time and in sharing ideas. Robin allowed me access to his remarkable collection of medieval European coins, several of which feature in the book, and Dr Joseph Bispham, similarly, offered wise counsel and images from his collection. I have also received help and advice from Jennifer Adam and Eleanor Paton at the Bank of England Museum, Dr Martin Allen and Dr Richard Kelleher at the Fitzwilliam Museum, Marion Avon, Pamela Hunter at Hoare's Bank, Harry Mernick, Dr John Rainey, Alan Kelly, Stephen Raw and Sir John Wheeler.

Despite his many other commitments, especially in the centenary year marking the end of the First World War, Sir Hew Strachan agreed to write the Foreword, a selfless act characteristic of his generous nature. The book has been designed with flair by Nigel Tudman of Tuch Design. Through several projects stretching over more than twenty years, he has been imaginative and accommodating. My colleague, Graham Dyer, has again gone above and beyond the call of duty in reading through successive drafts and contributing an abundance of helpful suggestions which have enriched the narrative. I could not, finally, have found the time to complete this book without the support of my wife, Laura, who has allowed it to intrude into weekends and evenings, offering much-needed encouragement at every opportunity.